yummy baby

jane clarke

yummy baby

Every parent's guide to nutritious food for babies and toddlers

foreword by Jools Oliver

photography by Deirdre Rooney

MITCHELL BEAZLEY

Dedicated to my gorgeous Maya

Yummy Baby

First published in Great Britain in 2007 by Mitchell Beazley
An imprint of Octopus Publishing Group Limited,
2–4 Heron Quays, London E14 4JP.
An Hachette Livre UK Company.

A CIP catalogue record for this book is available from the British Library.

ISBN: 978 1 845333 31 7

The information, advice and views expressed in this book are those of the author
and based on her expertise as a qualified dietitian and practising nutritionist.
While the information and advice in this book is as accurate as possible at the time
of going to press, no legal responsibility or liability can be accepted by the author,
publisher or editors for any errors nor for any consequences arising from the use
thereof or from the information contained therein. This book is not intended as a
substitute for professional nutritional, dietetic or medical advice where necessary
and appropriate and you are advised to consult a health professional for specific
information in all matters relating to the health of your child and yourself.

Commissioning Editor: Rebecca Spry
Art Director: Tim Foster
Designer: Nicky Collings
Prop Stylist: Isabel De Cordova
Home Economists: Louise Mackaness, Sarah Lewis
Photographer: Deirdre Rooney
Editors: Annie Lee, Martyn Page
Production: Lucy Carter
Proofreader: Philippa Bell
Index: Diana LeCore

Typeset in Clarendon

Printed and bound in China

contents

foreword

After reading through Jane's latest cracker of a book I can only say that there are really no more questions that I need to ask regarding health, wellbeing and nutrition for babies and beyond.

It is very rare – in fact impossible – to find a book that really does tell mums- and dads-to-be everything they need to know to get the best possible start for their new and growing family. Even though I have long passed – well, just passed – that newborn baby stage when your head is constantly filled with complicated unanswered questions regarding everything from breast-feeding to baby constipation, I still find Jane's book fascinating and essential reading.

What I loved most when reading *Yummy Baby* is the uncomplicated, unfussy way in which it is written and laid out. When you are a new mum the last thing you need to read and refer to is a heavily-laden book full of complicated, confusing and, quite frankly, boring information, which is also often old-fashioned and unclear in its advice. Jane's book takes you on a simple journey from the newborn through to the toddler stage. There is even a section devoted to parents, which is fantastic as there is always a danger that you get so wrapped up in 'babyland' that you totally ignore your own needs. And without the parent functioning properly, it all falls apart – believe me, I've been there!

Nutrition is so unbelievably important for all of us: eating well and, most importantly, understanding your food arms you with the most powerful knowledge, and this, I believe, enables you to lead a well-balanced, happy and fulfilled life. That is why it is so important to learn about and appreciate healthy food from a young age – it's all synonymous with excellent wellbeing.

With Jane's book you get a balanced, unpretentious and non-patronizing view of all things baby. I especially liked the boxes in each chapter laying out the facts clearly, with great advice and easy-to-read specifics and essentials. The recipes are fantastic – new and fresh – and I have just tweaked my shopping list to include Greek yoghurt; the girls are in for a treat this weekend – fish pie!

It would have been fab if this book had been written when my children were still small babies. A book packed with this much information is like gold dust to me – I have learnt so much from it and, who knows, maybe we might be using it for another little baby Oliver in the future!

Jools Oliver

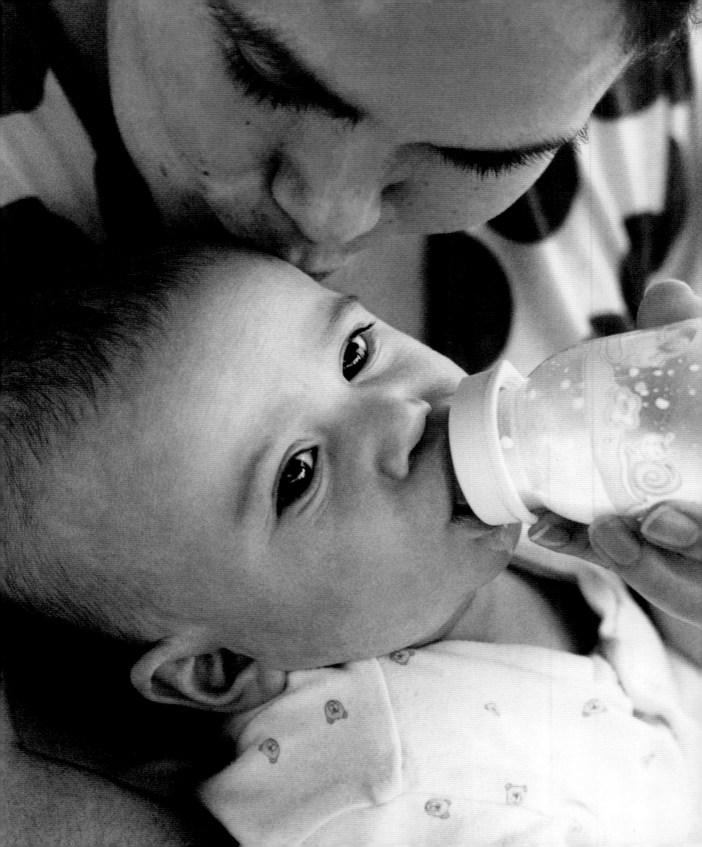

introduction

The arrival of a new generation is an opportunity to gain a better education about food, and therefore better futures for us all. Food education begins long before lessons in counting and the alphabet. It begins as soon as something other than the mother's milk passes an infant's lips.

And it begins at home.

If there are two things I've learned since becoming a mum, the first is that we can only try our best to get things right; the second is that it's often impossible to do everything we set ourselves in any one day. On a good day, I manage half.

Life is pretty complicated, whether we're juggling parenting with a stressful work environment or coping with the manic routines of family life. Our morning routine is like a military operation, as we move quickly from task to task in the hope that we'll get out of the door with all the right things in our bags – changes of clothing, enough nappies, socks and pants (I sometimes have to check myself!). Then we have to get to wherever the baby is spending the day – with a childminder or at a nursery – without storming along the road like mad people. And then the official day starts!

On top of this, food has become tricky. We're offered so many types. On the one hand, sophisticated food marketing seems to give us information, but on the other things can be a bit complicated when we try to work out whether or not something is good for our families.

What further confuses parents is the advice offered by friends and family and the messages from the media and government: 'Yes, you should buy organic.' 'No, you shouldn't, local's better.' 'Eggs are safe to eat.' 'No, they're not.' 'It's important to watch fat grams.' 'Oh, but isn't it all about the right sort of fat, so shouldn't you be scrutinizing labels for trans fats?' 'Incorporate at least five superfoods in your child's daily diet for them to stand any chance of being healthy.' Aaagh! Maybe about one per cent of this advice is useful and can be very welcome (at times), but often we wish they'd keep it to themselves, and we weren't overloaded with so much information.

From the minute you find out you're pregnant, you'll want to eat foods rich in nutrients that you know can help your unborn baby to grow well. For some, sickness can make pregnancy hell. But any of you mums who are still struggling with sickness after the 12th to 16th week of pregnancy should know that it will get better – and be reassured that even if you're not managing to eat a well-balanced, superfood-rich diet, your baby will be fine. Babies take many of the vitamins, minerals, proteins and other nutrients they need from your body – nourishment you've stored up over the years. It's you who could end up feeling drained after the birth, but luckily that can be fixed pretty quickly.

YUMMY BABY MAKES IT EASY

Our family food environment seems to be continually changing – but what you'll learn from this book is that although messages, articles and labels may confuse you, a little knowledge will help you cut through the jargon. It's true, certain advice will vary as your baby gets older, but the foundations of what a baby's needs won't.

You can easily become overloaded with expert advice from parenting books and the media. Many books give menus, exact amounts that your baby should be eating and when, as well as suggestions about how to manage his minutely-balanced-to-the-nth-degree meals. Reference books can be useful, but I want to challenge them on a few points.

Yummy Baby isn't full of tables and charts. That's because once you have the right information about the basic types and quantities of food your baby should be eating, you'll have the confidence to make food decisions according to your own needs and your baby's.

YOUR CHILD'S FOOD DAY

I don't agree that children need special foods or special drinks. We can feed them, from a few months old through to 3 years and beyond, with foods the whole family can eat. It's true that at certain stages their bodies can't digest or tolerate certain foods, but on the whole healthy babies can enjoy the same foods we do.

If children eat food that's different from the rest of the family it encourages them to think that there should be lots of foods on offer for them to choose from. Often, children are fussy eaters simply because they have always been able to get what they want if they kick up enough fuss. If children eat the same foods as their parents, they immediately join in with family meals. And mealtimes are not just about stocking up our bodies with the right fuel, they're also a time for a family to communicate and for a child to learn valuable skills.

I don't want to go on endlessly about the 'olden days', but they certainly got a lot of things right (not everything, of course) – one being that children ate when they sat down for meals. OK, until they are 2 years old, children seldom eat enough at mealtimes and need a couple of nutritious snacks during the day. After this stage, snacks may be needed occasionally – when you have a particularly long day, perhaps, or are away from home. But on a day-to-day

basis, try to get away from giving them. On car journeys, sitting in doctors' waiting-rooms, on trains, in prams – we seem to have got into the mindset that children must always have a little something to eat or drink to keep them happy. Food is often used as a pacifier, to make up for any shortfall in parenting skills we were never taught.

We've all had times when our kids' behaviour or our mood means we're pushed to our limits in a public place. But putting something into the child's mouth to solve the problem now seems to have become the norm. We are having huge problems with children becoming overweight from an early age because they're eating too much. The simple fact is that if your baby is brought up to be comforted by having food or drink, the likelihood is that he'll become overweight.

If you're eating well yourself, you can incorporate your child's eating into your own healthy routine. Eat well and you're less likely to be exhausted, so you can enjoy your child and have the energy to ensure that food is something that's fun (or at least do-able without a frown on your face or a glass of wine in each hand!). It's true that I don't have fun at every meal I eat with my daughter Maya. Some meals can be difficult when she plays up and doesn't want to eat the food we're eating (though less so now she's 4 than when she was 3). Getting your children, especially when they're over 12 months, to eat healthily can be a battle, but of all the battles parents need to win, it's one of the most important.

WHY FOOD MATTERS

What you feed your child during his first 3 years is incredibly important for sustaining growth and development. We have learnt so much more about the influence of the early diet on health later in life that parents now want to sow the right seeds to protect their child's health.

Laying good nutritional foundations will help to build up a healthy immune system, a strong, fit body and give a happy, contented child who can concentrate and learn. And if we start them off eating well, we have a better chance of avoiding screaming food-battles when they're older.

Of course, as soon as society, friends and peer pressure start exerting their influences on your child, battles, such as getting them to eat vegetables, can rear their heads once more, but a positive start will stand him in good stead.

MY EXPERIENCE AS A MUM

My daughter Maya came to me as a tiny, frail baby of 15 months and has blossomed into the most beautiful, strong, tall, healthy 4-year-old. Contrary to what many journalists have expected when they've asked me what special foods I had to feed her (she had rickets and was suffering from extreme malnourishment), I haven't spent the last three years donning my white coat as a nutritionist mum, weighing out special foods for her to eat. We have simply eaten family food together. I've made sure the food has contained enough of the right vitamins, minerals and other nutrients, but I've just done what any other parent strives to achieve – given her healthy food that she's grown to love (most of the time!).

Of course we've had our moments. But I hope what you'll learn from my experiences, both as a mum and as a nutritionist who's treated many children and families, that blips are normal and you can get through them. There are many great highs, too, when you see your children thriving on every level, when they tuck into something yummy and can't get enough of it, and when they say, 'This is delicious, Mum!'

HOW TO USE YUMMY BABY

I've divided the book into sections that you can dip into when you need facts, inspiration and reassurance. You'll find tricks of the trade that I've learned from working with different children with all sorts of health problems in my nutritional practice, and also things I've learned being a mum to Maya.

The recipes can all be cooked for the whole family – even puréed vegetables can be delicious as a grown-up meal, with crumbled feta cheese or roast chicken, for instance. Some dishes contain ingredients you may think are too complicated or sophisticated for a baby or toddler, but children don't have to have bland food. They might like something easy, such as rice and banana, but there's no reason why they can't also have a little chilli, garlic or spices virtually as soon as you start weaning. The recipes are either quick to prepare or

they freeze well, so that you can save time on another occasion – by simply defrosting a bag of risotto base, for example, and throwing in some peas or other ingredients to turn it into a nutritious meal.

In my recipes you'll find butter, cream, jam, white bread and other foods that have been demonized. I've included these 'bad' foods partly because it can be nutritious to have them as part of your child's eating day, but also because I would much rather a child had a good-quality jam and white bread sandwich than a processed meat or cheese dish. Just because the food label says it contributes valuable calcium, parents have been misled into thinking it is good. We don't need these special processed foods!

You will see some ingredients mentioned here that you may not be familiar with, such as pure fruit spreads and fruit concentrates, but you can buy these in good health-food stores, online, or even in some supermarkets. It's only if we create a demand for such nutritious ingredients that all the supermarkets will start stocking them.

But back to the beginning: your eating journey as a family starts right after birth, when you face the decision of breast- versus bottle-feeding, so milk feeds for newborn babies is the subject of the first chapter.

milk

Most mums have decided whether to breast-feed by the time they give birth. Breast-feeding doesn't suit everyone; it's great if you can do it, but if you can't don't worry! That said, even if you only breast-feed for a few days, it's a good way to bond with your baby. It also helps your womb to shrink towards its normal size. And since milk draws on fat deposits laid down during pregnancy, your body is more likely to return to its pre-pregnancy state fast.

Breast-feeding clearly makes a big difference to babies' health. The use of formula instead of breast-feeding is associated with a higher risk of hospitalization with diarrhoea and vomiting, respiratory infections, ear and urinary tract infections, allergies and associated problems. There is an increased risk of developing insulin-dependent diabetes, being overweight and having higher blood pressure as a child, and of breast cancer in mothers who don't breast-feed. But this doesn't mean all, or even most, formula-fed babies are sick and all breast-fed babies are healthy.

Breast-feeding

benefits of breast-feeding

✓ Breast-feeding provides everything your baby needs to develop and thrive for his first 6 months.

✓ Breast milk is always available fresh, usually in the right amounts (apart from when you're having problems producing enough) and at the right temperature for your baby.

✓ Breast milk is a living fluid, containing active cells that mop up bacteria and viruses, and antibodies tailored to fight infections. These are missing from formula.

✓ Breast-feeding provides your baby with an immune boost, as his own immunity is still developing.

✓ Breast-feeding is much cheaper than bottle-feeding.

✓ Breast-feeding is good for the environment; it does not need processing, packaging or transporting.

✓ Your breasts are in tune with the temperature and environment, so if it's hot and your baby feeds more frequently, he will receive more thirst-quenching milk – clever!

✓ Breast-feeding requires lots of skin-to-skin contact, which babies need. It is a uniquely bonding experience – although you can ensure that bottle-feeding involves lots of cuddling, which is no hardship.

✓ Breast-feeding doesn't need any equipment unless you have to be separated, when you can express breast milk for later use. In contrast, formula, bottles, teats and sterilizing equipment must be bought, the sterilizer carefully mixed with the right amount of pure, boiled water, and bottles must be kept scrupulously clean.

✓ Most mums find breast-feeding is easier than bottle-feeding after the initial physical adjustment.

✓ Babies who are breast-fed have much less smelly nappies.

Note: A study in Finland found that babies fed exclusively on mothers' milk beyond 6 months (the usual time to introduce solid food) may have an increased risk of developing allergies, food hypersensitivity, etc. So it seems it's great to breast-feed for the first 6 months but after that, in order for a baby to develop an appropriate immune system that's not too sensitive, we should introduce other foods.

breast-feeding basics

You should receive plenty of help and support from your midwife or breast-feeding counsellor straight after your baby's birth. This is a crucial time for learning how to position your baby so that he gets enough milk and you avoid sore and damaged nipples, which can become infected.

It'll probably take time to get used to having a baby feeding from you. But you *will* get used to it and gain the confidence to follow your baby's cues. For instance, he may want to take milk from both breasts every feed, perhaps with a natural break in between. But if he doesn't drink at all, or for very long, from one breast, offer the same breast the next time he wants a feed.

THE FIRST FEW DAYS
The first milk you produce after your baby is born is called colostrum. At between 2 and 5 days after the birth, your milk 'comes in'. This is because prolactin, the milk-making hormone, starts working on your breasts as soon as the placenta is delivered. If you don't breast-feed, production slows down and then stops. You continue producing milk only if it's removed from your breasts – that's how your body knows your baby wants it.

WHEN YOUR MILK COMES IN
At first, your baby will feed a lot – maybe 10 to 15 times over 24 hours – and you may not be able to predict when he will want to sleep. This is how your body adapts to producing the amount of milk he needs. You're unlikely to get into a routine before he's at least 6 weeks old; he'll probably stop and start and can take longer than you might expect. But as time goes on, feeds tend to become more predictable (though there may still be occasional days when all he wants to do is breast-feed).

SIGNS THAT IT'S GOING WELL
Breast-feeding seems a bit slapdash in comparison to the structured bottle-feeding routines. But your baby will soon tell you when it's going well – and when it's not.

Signs that tell you when everything is going well include:
- your baby should seem happy and contented after a good feed
- your baby shouldn't fight when you put him on and take him off your breast
- your baby will gain weight
- your baby will have several wet nappies each day
- your baby will do soft yellow poos
- your nipples and breasts shouldn't get sore.

IF BABY DOESN'T GAIN MUCH WEIGHT
If your baby is not gaining much weight, don't panic. Just ask your midwife for advice. You might not be eating enough, perhaps because you're engrossed in

your baby or are simply too tired to eat properly. And tiredness in itself can impact on milk production, so make sure you're not overdoing it.

SEVERE REACTION TO BREAST MILK

Occasionally a baby has a more severe reaction to his mum's breast milk, for instance he might develop a skin rash or hives, have difficulty breathing, wheezing or congestion, or his stools might turn green or contain mucus. In all these cases, seek medical help.

STORING EXPRESSED MILK

You can freeze unwanted breast milk in sterile freezing bags for up to 6 months or keep it in the fridge for up to 24 hours. If breast-feeding is taking a long time to get established, freeze your expressed milk for later.

THINKING OF GIVING UP?

Most mums hit an occasional problem with breast-feeding. The important thing is to ask for advice before you give up, as it may be something minor, and it's much easier to correct small problems while you're still trying to breast-feed, even if you're only producing a little, than to stop and then try to re-start.

Sometimes the problem can't be solved, for example, your baby may not be able to take enough nourishing milk from you, or you may be ill and have to go on drugs that mustn't be transferred to him. There are many reasons that can make it impossible to continue breast-feeding.

'You can freeze unwanted breast milk in sterile freezing bags for up to 6 months or keep it in the fridge for up to 24 hours.'

your diet when breast-feeding

All you need is a good well-balanced diet with a couple of tweaks. If you eat well, you will produce milk that's nutritionally well-rounded and you'll be less drained by the whole 'being a new parent' thing and the added element of a baby taking nutrients from your body.

YOUR NUTRITION

On page 69 you'll see what a child's day should look like in terms of nutrition; the same balance applies to you.

YOUR APPETITE

Your appetite might change while you're breast-feeding, both in terms of the types of foods you want and the times you want to eat. Mums commonly need smaller meals more often and/or feel hungry after they've eaten. You might want a larger breakfast than you're used to, or you might eat a cooked meal in the middle of the day and something lighter and quicker in the evening, when you're tired. Just see what works for you.

Eating with your partner if he comes back later wanting a big cooked meal can put a spanner in the works. Why not see if you can persuade him to have his main meal at lunchtime – then you can choose simple things to prepare in the evening, such as an omelette, soup, cold cuts of meat, or bread and cheese. The important thing is to put you and your baby first – after all, you may only be breast-feeding for a few months. And it's much better

for everyone concerned for you to eat well and feel well, in a routine that suits you, than to be forever eating late and feeling lousy, resentful and grumpy!

YOUR WATER INTAKE

Breast-feeding mums should drink between 2.5 and 3 litres of water a day.

HOW MANY EXTRA CALORIES YOU NEED

Your baby takes nutrients such as vitamins, minerals, fat, protein and carbohydrate from your milk, so you need to eat enough to produce good milk and to satisfy your needs too. But you don't need to eat for two. The Department of Health says that you need an extra 450 calories a day for the first month, 530 for the second month, and 570 thereafter. But I think, as do many, that these figures are too high; I recommend you need an extra 300–400 calories for the first 3 months and an extra 400 or so calories thereafter. This translates into an extra small meal, such as a hearty cheese sandwich, or a large banana and a couple of buttery shortbread biscuits, or a couple of thick, creamy yoghurts with some dried fruits.

This might sound like a lot, but if you bear in mind that non-breast-feeding women should drink 2.5 litres a day, you can see that the extra half litre for all your milk demands isn't much.

Some women feel fine not drinking this much, but most end up feeling more tired than they need be, and ratty, headachy and constipated as well. You can tell by the colour of your urine whether you're drinking enough water – dark, smelly urine says that you're not; it should be a pale straw colour.

Try to stagger this water intake during the day, rather than downing it all at once, as this can help your kidneys to hold on to the water rather than you peeing it straight out.

TAP WATER

I am a tap water rather than a bottled water drinker for several reasons. The water that comes out of our taps is well regulated. OK, in some areas of the country it can taste a little strange, but this is less noticeable if you pour the water into a jug and pop it into the fridge for a while. (Don't worry about hormones and other scare stories – it's perfectly safe to drink our tap water, and its bacterial and chemical composition is generally subject to much tighter regulation than bottled water. If you're worried, contact your water supplier and ask for a safety check.)

WATER FILTERS

A filter jug may make your tap water taste better. Follow the instructions properly and change the filter regularly, because an old filter will not do its job and will also increase the bacterial content of your water. You should not use filtered water for making up infant formula, as the filter can change the mineral balance of the water, making it unsuitable for babies.

BOTTLED WATER

If you still prefer bottled water, choose one labelled 'natural mineral water' because this is subject to the strictest regulations. Be sure to drink it within 24 hours of opening to prevent the proliferation of bacteria, which can cause stomach upsets.

Check that it doesn't contain excessive levels of salt; ideally choose water with a maximum of 20mg of sodium per litre – a moderate level would be between 20mg and 200mg of sodium, but anything above this is far too salty, particularly for young children.

STILL VERSUS SPARKLING WATER

Sparkling water does not cause cancer, cellulite, or anything else suggested in the mad stories I hear around – it's water, just that. And I love sparkling water for a change, especially chilled with ice. But if you like to drink it, watch out for the level of gassiness (this varies, and some overly bubbly ones can affect people who suffer from IBS or heartburn).

TEA AND COFFEE

A cup of tea can restore my sanity. And if you're thinking that tea and coffee don't hydrate the body at all, this isn't entirely the case. If you drink a little at a time (don't drink more than a couple of cups in one go), you should feel refreshed and well hydrated. However, it is still important to drink plenty of water as well – especially if you're not used to consuming caffeine.

It's usually fine to have up to 400mg of caffeine a day (about what you'd get in four mugs of coffee – see the chart right) when breast-feeding. That said, caffeine, even in small amounts, can make sensitive mums feel more stressed and jittery, and can keep them awake at the wrong moments. Heavy caffeine drinkers may also find that their baby seems to be awake a lot or a little tetchy.

I advise that you keep your intake down to two cups of tea or coffee a day. There are healthy decaffeinated teas and coffees now – best to choose ones that have used water or carbon dioxide to remove the caffeine, as I feel these are the healthiest.

CORDIAL AND SQUASH
While there's nothing wrong with a little good cordial or squash added to water, it's best to keep your intake of sugars, acids and artificial sweeteners down. Sugars can affect your energy levels, weight, and teeth. Acids (in fizzy drinks, for instance, either with sugars or sweeteners) can also affect your teeth and are not good for bone health. Sweeteners alone don't really adversely affect your energy, weight or teeth but many people, myself included, prefer to

CAFFEINE LEVELS IN FOOD AND DRINK
Consume no more than 400mg a day

- 1 average-size mug of instant coffee contains 100mg caffeine
- 1 average-size cup of instant coffee contains 75mg caffeine
- 1 average-size cup of brewed coffee contains 100mg caffeine
- 1 average-size cup of tea contains 50mg caffeine
- 1 can of 'energy' drink contains up to 80mg caffeine
- 1 chocolate bar (50g) contains up to 50mg caffeine
- 1 can of cola contains up to 40mg caffeine

avoid them. See my list of good, safe (and sometimes therapeutic) herbal teas on page 25.

VITAMIN D SUPPLEMENTS
Although you can get most of the necessary vitamins and minerals you and your baby need from your diet, vitamin D falls into a grey area. We don't get enough of it in our diet to match our increased vitamin D requirement while we're producing such large volumes of milk. So take a supplement containing 10 micrograms (mcg) of vitamin D each day, in the form of a teaspoonful of cod-liver oil or a vitamin D capsule (available from health-food stores).

BREAST-FEEDING AND DIETING

The body will use the remaining fat that women tend to have after giving birth to produce milk. Don't diet while breast-feeding, as it can leave you depleted and exhausted and your milk lacking in sufficient nutrition.

Of course, exercise can help burn up some calories, produce endorphins and give you a break. Even just getting out of the house burns up calories. When my daughter Maya was little, on days when I was feeling exhausted and blue, I would go for a walk; just seeing other people, trees, and getting fresh air into my lungs made me feel much better. Don't set yourself mad gym routines while breast-feeding, though, as you could end up more exhausted!

'The body will use the remaining fat women tend to have after giving birth to produce milk.'

HERBAL TEAS

My favourite herbal teas which are safe to drink while breast-feeding are:

chamomile: Calms and de-stresses; flowers give sweetest flavour.

echinacea: Thought to help the immune system fight infection – but studies to back up claims are mixed.

elderflower: Fights fevers, and is thought to help build up the immune system – although research hasn't yet substantiated the claims.

fennel: Combats digestive problems such as bloating, stomach pain and cramps – one only needs to have a baby with wind, or suffer with IBS, to know its benefits.

ginger: Helps alleviate morning sickness, colds and digestive complaints such as wind, colic, indigestion, and constipation.

lemon verbena: A light, refreshing digestif; relieves bloating and wind.

nettle: Rich in minerals needed to keep healthy; thought to boost nursing mothers' milk production; may help relieve arthritic inflammation and pain.

peppermint: An effective digestif; soothes coughs; relieves faintness and hysteria (supposedly!).

vervain: Also known as verbena, this helps alleviate symptoms of PMS, stress and nervous exhaustion; aids digestion; bolsters the nervous system; relieves headaches and migraines; speeds recuperation from illness – what a herb! It's also delicious and very easy to grow.

Many mums are thankful they no longer need to avoid all the classic pregnancy no-no's, such as blue and soft cheese. You can eat away! But there are a couple of things to watch, the first being fish.

FISH YOU CAN EAT

Fish is rich in proteins and good oils, and is therefore healthy for you and your baby when you're breast-feeding. But you need to watch the type and quantity of fish you eat. You can eat as much white, non-oily fish, such as cod, halibut and plaice, as you like.

FISH YOU SHOULD LIMIT

Stick to no more than two portions a week of oily fish, such as trout, salmon, mackerel, sardines and herrings, because they contain tiny amounts of pollutants, some of which will pass into your breast milk. The Food Standards Agency defines a portion as 140g (5oz).

You can safely eat up to one portion of shark, swordfish and marlin a week.

During pregnancy, up to four medium-sized tins of tuna a week is the safe limit; this amount can be increased when breast-feeding (but who can eat more than this anyway?). Fresh tuna, however, needs to be treated like other oily fish. This is because tuna only counts as an oily fish when it is fresh; when it is canned the omega-3 oil levels are reduced to levels similar to those in white fish. Consequently, although canned tuna is a healthy option, it doesn't have the same health benefits as fresh oily fish.

REACTIONS TO VEGETABLES

You may find that your baby reacts badly – say has an upset tummy, complains or whinges more – after you've eaten vegetables such as cauliflower or cabbage. But every child is different, and plenty of mums have munched their way through the vegetable patch and had no problem with their babies. In the case of a severe reaction, seek medical help.

PEANUTS AND ALLERGIES

Peanuts are one of the most common causes of food allergy, affecting about one per cent of the population. This doesn't sound a lot, but the allergic reaction to peanuts is very severe (it can cause anaphylaxis, which is very serious and can be life-threatening).

So tread carefully with the peanut issue if you, the baby's father, brothers or sisters have a food allergy or other allergic condition such as hay fever, asthma and/or eczema. If this sounds like your family, avoid eating peanuts and peanut products while you're breast-feeding and while you're introducing solid foods (see page 208), as this could increase the risk of your baby developing an allergy.

Also avoid giving peanuts and peanut products to babies and toddlers because they are at higher risk of developing

before they are 3 years old. If you think your child might be allergic to peanuts, speak to your GP.

WHEN PEANUTS ARE SAFE

If you have no such family history, eating peanuts is fine. One of the main reasons why breast-feeding is so great is because it's the first time you transfer all sorts of foods and immunological cells to your baby. Most of the time you want to expose him to tiny amounts of the proteins found in foods, as this triggers him to develop an appropriate tolerance of the proteins in these foods, which are responsible for allergic reactions. So by eating peanuts you will be helping your baby not to develop allergies to them.

ALCOHOL

Alcohol, like caffeine (and nicotine), passes from your blood into your breast milk. While some research shows that alcohol can disrupt the release of two key hormones responsible for milk production, oxytocin and prolactin, the odd glass of wine, beer or other alcohol is fine while breast-feeding. Oh, and by the way, the old wives' tale of alcohol being good for milk production is nonsense. The best way to deal with having a glass of wine and breast-feeding is to feed your baby first and drink second.

'You no longer need to avoid all the classic pregnancy no-nos such as soft cheese; you can eat away!'

bottle-feeding

bottle-feeding basics

I understand how disappointing it can be if you can't breast-feed your baby – and some of you may even feel guilty if you don't want to – but sometimes the only way forward is to use a formula feed. Millions of children, including my daughter, have been brought up perfectly healthily and lovingly with formula milk in a bottle.

BOTTLE-FEEDING FROM DAY ONE

There are all sorts of reasons why bottle-feeding is the only practical answer for some. Not everyone is able to breast-feed, or wants to. I couldn't breast-feed my daughter because I adopted her when she was 15 months old. Many mothers have to work.

Some mums manage to express milk to be given to the baby while they're away, but others just can't do that, perhaps because of illness or for other reasons. None of these reasons are bad. And although I wasn't able to pass on the immunological protection and other physiological benefits by breast-feeding my daughter, we developed an incredibly strong, loving and nutritious way of life for her using formula milk. It's a question of making sure your child benefits in as many ways as possible.

MOVING FROM BREAST TO BOTTLE

If, like many mums, you switch from breast to bottle, try to give yourself plenty of time to make the change, as the two of you will need time to get used to it. Give yourself a couple of weeks so that your milk supply decreases gradually, during which time your baby can get used to the feel of a teat and the taste of formula milk.

If you have a partner, suggest that he does the bottle-feeding so that your baby doesn't smell your milk. I'd start with a bottle once a day, when your baby is bright and attentive, then next day introduce a second bottle at a different time. Eventually, alternate breast-feeds with a bottle, and finally limit the breast-feeds to last thing at night and first thing in the morning, before cutting them out completely.

choosing the right formula milk

Formula milks are usually dried, and you reconstitute them with cooled boiled water – although 'ready-to-feed' formula is also available in cartons and sachets, which can be useful when travelling and for keeping in your bag for emergencies.

You need to choose a recognized infant formula. The main types of formula for babies under 6 months are listed and described below.

WHEY-BASED MILK

This is the most common type of formula milk. It is based on cow's milk and is normally recommended as the best choice for bottle-fed babies from birth. The protein content has more whey in it than casein, which reflects breast milk's balance of these ingredients.

Most brands of formula milk have long-chain fatty acids in them as an added ingredient. This is marketed to parents as providing some of the 'extras' in breast milk that help with the development of the brain, but there's no conclusive evidence either way.

CASEIN-BASED MILK

This type of formula milk is suitable for babies from birth, although it's usually marketed as being for 'hungrier' babies, because the casein is less easily digestible than whey and is supposed to keep your baby feeling fuller for longer. Only use it if your health adviser or doctor has suggested it.

HYDROLYZED AND ELEMENTAL MILK

Some infant formula is hydrolyzed, which means it has been treated in a way that breaks up the proteins into small pieces. This can make the proteins easier to absorb, and can be suitable for babies who are usually allergic to cow's milk. This type of milk is available on prescription. Examples of hydrolyzed infant formulas are Nutramigen or Pregestimil. A few milk-allergic children react even to these formulas and so may need an elemental formula, which has had its proteins and different elements within the milk made easy for highly allergic babies to absorb.

SOYA MILK

This is used for babies who can't tolerate cow's milk formula, usually because of lactose intolerance. You don't need to give your baby soya formula (or, indeed, any of the other baby formulas, other than the classic whey-based feeds) unless your doctor or health visitor has told you to. It's important to make the right choice. You may be able to get soya milk on prescription.

GOAT'S MILK

Parents who have an issue with cow's milk can find themselves wondering if goat's milk formulas are an OK choice or better for their baby. The simple answer is no. This is because goat's milk formula and goat's milk follow-on formula don't

SOYA INFANT FORMULA: IS IT SAFE?

Some parents have concerns about the presence of phytoestrogens in soya formula. Phytoestrogens are oestrogen-like substances that occur naturally in many plants, including soya. There is some unease that a large intake of these substances could have an adverse effect on a baby's hormonal development. Because babies weigh so little, they will take in higher levels of phytoestrogens than adults or children who eat some soya products as part of a mixed diet. It's a hotly debated issue, not least because the soya industry is powerful at lobbying and the soya business is huge and exceedingly valuable.

The evidence

Research on animals has shown that large amounts of phytoestrogens affect the development of their reproductive organs and fertility. But there's no evidence from the limited number of studies on humans that there would be similar effects on us. So it's not clear whether soya-based infant formula could affect a baby's reproductive development or not.

The advice

I support the Food Standards Agency advice that, until a full review of the evidence has been completed, soya formula should only be given to babies under 12 months in exceptional circumstances.

have all the nutrients, vitamins and minerals your baby needs. Also, the proteins in goat's milk are similar to those in cow's milk, and both have similar amounts of lactose, so babies who are intolerant of, or allergic to, cow's milk or who have lactose intolerance are just as likely to react badly to goat's milk formula. For these reasons, infant milks based on goat's milk are no longer available in this country.

SOYA INFANT FORMULA AND LACTOSE INTOLERANCE

I did, as many parents do, give my daughter soya infant formula because she was lactose intolerant. But before doing the same with your baby, you should discuss it with your doctor because it needs to be clear whether your baby's problem is with lactose or with cow's milk protein, in which case one of the hydrolyzed formulas may be more suitable. If you do end up using soya formula, when your baby reaches 12 months (when he's eating a mixed diet), use a combination of soya milk, rice, and oat milk as it's good not to overdo one type of lactose-free milk.

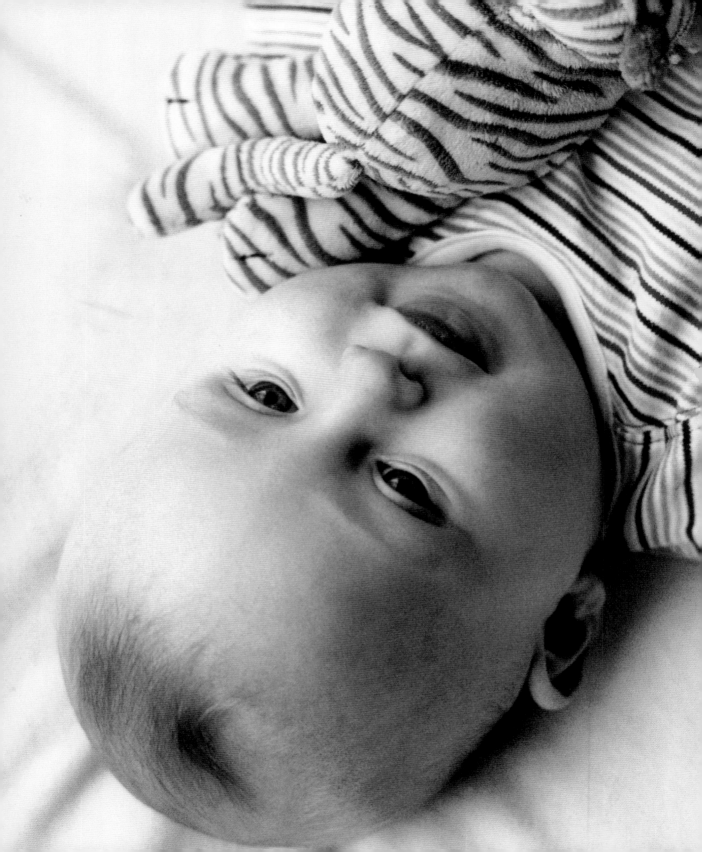

FOLLOW-ON MILK

Follow-on milks are specifically formulated for your baby after the age of 6 months. They can be used as a comforting drink or in dishes, with cereal in the morning for instance. They contain more iron and protein than milks designed for the first 6 months – but if your baby is eating well and you are including some iron- and protein-rich foods in his diet, you can use standard infant formula or some other milk instead. Ordinary cow's milk isn't right as a drink for babies under 12 months old, because it contains too much of some nutrients and not enough of others; you can use it in dishes, but not as a drink.

ORGANIC MILK

Organic formula is fine, but I believe it is not necessary. Non-organic baby formulas are nutritious and perfectly healthy for your child – not full of the hormones and pesticides that some parents worry about. But the cost difference is pretty small, so it's your choice.

MILK INTOLERANCE OR ALLERGIES

If your baby has (or you think he has) an intolerance or allergy to milk of any sort, see your doctor or heath visitor, who will be able to help you get the best advice (see page 206).

OTHER MILKS

Oat, rice and nut (such as almond) milks, although nutritious in their own right, and delicious, are not nutritionally complete enough to be given as a substitute for infant formula and shouldn't pass your baby's lips before he's 6 months old.

VITAMIN OR MINERAL DROPS

Infant formulas include all the necessary vitamins, minerals, etc. that your baby needs during his first 6 months, so you don't need to give him anything extra.

'Follow-on milks contain more iron and protein than milks designed for the first 6 months.'

how to prepare formula milk

STERILIZING EQUIPMENT

Keep all feeding equipment clean – you must sterilize between uses for the first 6 months. Formula-fed babies don't get the same protection from infection as breast-fed babies, and milk is the perfect breeding ground for bacteria, so it is important to be vigilant.

CHOICE OF WATER

Some mums may think bottled water is better since they prefer it themselves. But this isn't the case. It's best to empty out the kettle and use freshly run water from a tap – our tap water is highly regulated. Bottled water or reboiled tap water (or water treated with a water softener) may have high levels of minerals such as sodium that could be harmful to your baby.

You should never use filtered water for making up infant formula, as the filter can change the mineral balance of the water, making it unsuitable for babies. Also, unless you use a fresh filter, you could be giving your baby water with higher numbers of bacteria.

If you don't trust what looks like manky tap water, bottled water will be fine, as long as the label says that it's suitable for infant feeding (check with the manufacturer if it doesn't). Look for a bottled water containing less than 20mg sodium per litre. Bottled water still needs to be boiled for babies to make it bacteriologically safe.

WARMING THE MILK

Warm the milk in a pan of hot water rather than in a microwave. Microwaves can heat the milk too much from the inside, so it may be too hot even if the bottle feels cool on the outside. If you have no choice, heat it for a shorter time, and remember that industrial microwaves are more powerful than domestic ones. Always shake the milk to distribute the heat evenly when you take it out of the microwave; let it rest and thoroughly check on the back of your hand that it is body temperature before feeding it to your baby.

PREPARING MILK IN ADVANCE

It's wise to make up your baby's milk just before he drinks it, as baby milk feeds made up in advance are at risk of contamination from food poisoning bacteria, such as salmonella or a bacteria called *E. sakazaki*. However, formula can be kept in the fridge for 24 hours.

One option is to take the feeding bottle of hot water with you in a keep-warm insulated bag. Measure out the right number of scoops of baby milk into a separate lidded container and take this with you as well – when you're ready to feed, the water in the bottle will still be warm enough to mix with your powder for a fresh drink. I used to do this, especially at night, to minimize the chance of my waking up too much to be able to grab some more sleep when Maya

STERILIZING CHOICES:

- steam sterilizer (see left)

- sterilizing tablets or fluid

- wash bottles and then boil them for 25 minutes in a large covered pot

- once your baby is 12 months old, simply washing well in hot water with washing-up liquid is fine

- always use bottle and teat brushes when washing

had settled again. It also means you've got the milk right by you, so hopefully your baby will be crying for less time too.

Don't forget to check the temperature first by shaking a few drops on to your hand to check it's not too hot or too cold. It should feel warm.

'Bottled water or reboiled water may have high levels of minerals such as sodium that could be harmful to your baby.'

HOW MUCH FORMULA MILK TO FEED YOUR BABY EACH DAY

The rule of thumb is 2.5–2.7 ounces (oz) of formula per pound (lb) of body weight. So if your baby weighs 6lb, he should consume about 15–16oz of formula in a 24-hour period. If he weighs 10lb, he should have roughly 25–27oz in a 24-hour period. (This rule of thumb doesn't work with metric measures, so stick to imperial. But milk amounts will also be given from here on in metric as well as imperial.)

These are rough guidelines, and your health visitor will advise you on the right amount of formula for your baby as he grows. They don't apply to premature babies or babies with a low birth weight – again, ask your health visitor for advice.

How much formula your baby needs depends not only on his weight, but also on his age. Don't expect a newborn (or any baby, for that matter) to follow a schedule – some days he'll be hungry and guzzle; others he won't. This is normal. Appetites vary from baby to baby, and most babies vary from day to day and month to month. Your baby will feed as often as he needs to, as long as you learn to detect his cues and respond to them appropriately. Don't automatically give a bottle every time he cries – in time you'll learn to read his actions and work out if he's hungry or just needs attention.

One of the most confusing and emotive issues when you have well-meaning relatives and advisers around is how much milk you should give your baby. You worry that you're giving him too little and therefore depriving him of valuable nutrients; or you worry that you're giving him too much, and therefore setting him up for a lifetime of struggling with being overweight.

There is no single answer: it depends on your baby's age, weight, and whether you're feeding him only formula, or using it in combination with breast milk or solids.

YOUR BABY'S WEIGHT

When considering your baby's weight, look at yourselves as parents. Some babies aren't going to be big bruisers and are smaller eaters, and this is more likely if their parents are slight. I see a lot of anguish among mums who feel pressurized to feed their child more in order to pacify percentile charts and health visitors. (This is more common in mums who are breast-feeding, as they can feel an enormous pressure to get the whole milk thing right – and if their baby is lagging behind, they can feel horribly responsible, which leads to stress and possibly less milk production. See page 18 for what to do if your milk doesn't seem to be satisfying your baby.)

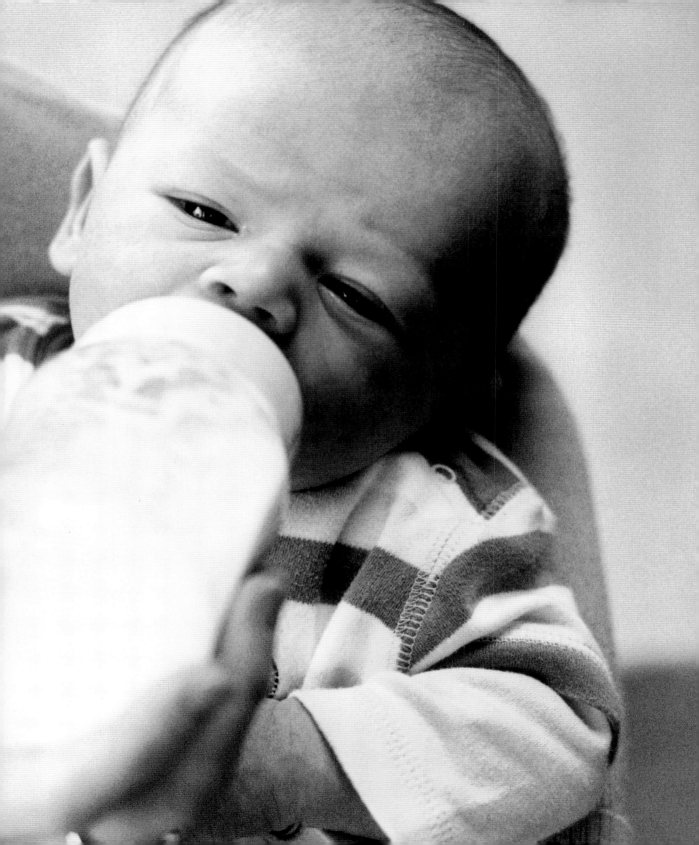

PROFESSIONAL HELP

If you are worried that your baby isn't taking enough milk, or is having too much, or seems to want more and more, or isn't interested in drinking from the bottle – anything, really – talk things through with your health visitor or doctor. They'd much rather act as reassuring voices now, and help you through little things, than be faced with a bigger problem later.

EXTRA WATER FOR BABIES

It's important to give your baby sips of cooled boiled water in between feeds, as this can prevent him from becoming dehydrated and gets him accustomed to the taste of plain water.

'How much milk you should give your baby depends on his age, weight and whether you're feeding him only formula.'

HOW MUCH FORMULA MILK TO FEED YOUR BABY EACH FEED

Newborn babies: If you're starting a newborn on formula, try giving him only 30–60ml/1–2fl oz at each feed for the first week.

1 month: By the time your baby is 1 month old, he will probably take 90–120ml/3–4fl oz at each feed, and will consume anywhere between 400 and 800ml/14–28fl oz in one day. You'll soon sense if he needs more – he'll finish the feed quickly and look around for second helpings!

2 to 6 months: You should be giving your baby 120–180ml/4–6fl oz at a feed, and he'll have anything from 700ml to over a litre/23–35fl oz a day.

6 months plus: You can feed your baby anything between 180 and 220ml/6–8fl oz at a feed, and his total formula intake should be roughly 900ml/32fl oz per day alongside his solid food.

As weaning progresses: Once you are adding solids, your baby's daily intake of formula milk should gradually decrease to about 720ml/24fl oz. Once he is established on solids, he should have approximately 600ml/20fl oz (1 pint) of formula milk per day alongside a varied diet until he's 12 months old.

how to wean

In no time your baby will be 6 months old and it will be time to introduce her to solids. The age to wean is not set in stone – some babies will grab bits of food off your plate at 5 months; others may look at food at 6 months and not be interested. Just bear in mind that around 6 months is the time to start.

My philosophy on weaning is that it should be about introducing your baby to your own diet, the foods you eat. But don't think you have to do a major shop for different foods to try immediately – it's just the start of a journey for your baby.

Taking the first steps towards getting your baby to eat real food can feel like jumping off a cliff. You'll have good days, when she tucks into everything, and others when you'll be lucky to get a spoon near her mouth. As long as you remember the few foods that need to be avoided to reduce the likelihood of allergies, the dangers of overloading her body with too much salt, or milk protein, and are careful over texture so she can't choke, you can wean in whatever way works for you.

the right time to wean

If you wait until 6 months before introducing solids, your baby's immune system will be at the stage when it can start responding to small amounts of food without the risk of an adverse reaction. This is particularly important if you have a family history of conditions such as asthma, eczema and hay fever, as the incidence of adverse reactions, allergies and coeliac disease (an adverse reaction to gluten – see page 207) decreases if you delay weaning until this time.

WHY WE WEAN AT 6 MONTHS

Neither breast milk nor formula alone can provide your baby with enough nutrients, particularly iron, once she reaches 6 months. Getting your baby to eat solid foods at this age is also an important part of developing her facial and mouth muscles for speech later on. And let's not forget that solid foods are a deliciously fun aspect of living – babies love copying little things we do, from smiling to picking things up, and we sometimes forget that food can be a great thing to play with, to tease you over, to test the boundaries. They watch you making food, then enjoy you sitting down and engaging with them.

EATING WITH YOUR BABY

Your baby will love simple things such as ground rice and pear to begin with. OK, you won't want to eat that, but as soon as possible I advocate feeding her little bits of the foods as you eat (with just a

WEANING EARLIER THAN 6 MONTHS

If you think your baby is ready to start tucking into solids before 6 months, talk this through with your health visitor. It can be fine to start earlier, but it's best to discuss it first. The Department of Health states that solid foods should not be introduced before the end of your baby's 4th month (20 weeks).

WHY NOT WEAN LATER THAN 6 MONTHS

Don't delay weaning longer than 6 months. If you do, your baby's immune system may not be able to develop an appropriate reaction to foods, so she could develop severe allergic reactions when she's older. Consider nuts, for example (see page 208) – unless you have an allergic family history, by introducing small amounts of peanuts (ground) and peanut products after the age of 6–7 months you actually help your baby's immune system to react in the right way and not develop a peanut allergy.

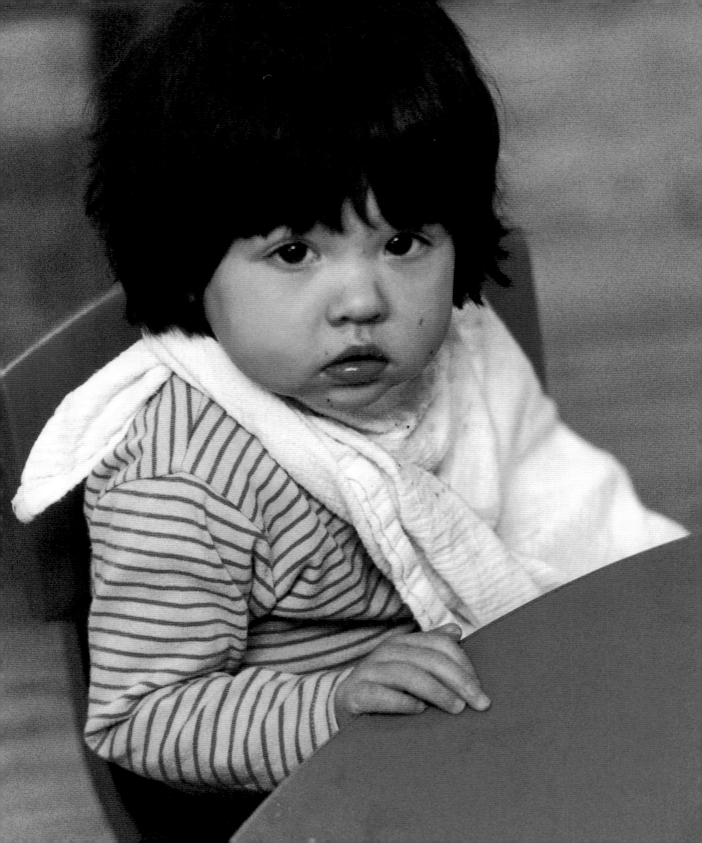

few safety precautions, such as making sure she can't choke, and not overloading her body with foods that are too grown-up, such as eggs, too soon). Forget special weaning foods and smiley carrot faces. There are delicious purées among my recipes (see pages 102–105), and they're foods all the family can eat too.

BENEFITS OF EATING TOGETHER
Having a baby is a great opportunity for the whole family to eat well, and things like not putting salt in food are good all round. Also, you are far more likely to bring up a child who is a non-fussy eater if you give her the foods you have prepared for yourself, so she sees you eating them. If you're putting the same food into your mouth, she will want to copy.

It's far easier to prepare just one set of meals for the day – the waitress-restaurant style is both madness and exhausting. I've seen families in which the parent cooks several different things each mealtime, for different children, and this just isn't on. You'll end up ragged, exhausted and fed up.

'Having a baby is a great opportunity for the whole family to eat well; things like not putting salt in food are good all round.'

MILK

Continue with your normal milk feed at 6 months.

BABY RICE

The first thing you need to get your baby to do is start swallowing something that's not a fluid, and something other than milk. Classic baby rice is a good, bland starter, mixed with either breast milk or formula – whichever she's used to. You can give her the rice on its own, or mix it with a little vegetable or fruit purée. Make the rice quite liquid with some breast milk or formula, or simple boiled water. Gradually, as your baby gets used to the feeling of something more solid in her mouth, you can reduce the amount of liquid you add.

VEGETABLE AND FRUIT PURÉES

Once you move on to fruit and vegetables, ensure they are properly cooked (all fruit and vegetables need cooking apart from those listed in the box, right) and puréed. It's fine to start babies on something fruity, but I'd be more inclined to go for a savoury vegetable hit. That way they don't get too used to sweet fruits and find it harder when you introduce something less sweet. Or try a combination of the two – carrot and apple purée, or avocado and apple. Avocado (strictly, a fruit) with puréed apple was a hit with my daughter.

FOODS YOUR BABY CAN EAT FROM 6 MONTHS AT-A-GLANCE

Vegetables
- All cooked vegetables are good from 6 months, so try to give your baby a variety. You may like to mash stronger-tasting vegetables, such as broccoli, green beans and peas, into some potato or sweet potato, or of course baby rice or oats. Shop-bought frozen vegetables and fruits are not only nutritious but can make your life easier. Just steam or microwave a few frozen vegetables and blend them to whatever consistency your baby likes. Cucumber does not need cooking.

Rice
- Baby rice.
- Well-cooked and mashed white rice.

Fruit
- Raw fruit – soft and ripe melon, avocado, peach, plums, bananas and figs are all OK raw or cooked.
- Cooked fruit – apples and pears are favourites. The only fruits to avoid are citrus fruits, berries, kiwi and pineapple.

FOOD ALLERGIES

It's best to introduce one food at a time at first, so that you can tell if your baby reacts adversely. But this isn't a fixed rule, and with children who don't have a high risk of allergy you can introduce new foods in combination or different foods every day if you prefer.

The incidence of food allergy in babies is very small – I think media hype has made parents think it's more common than it is. Also, the fact that we now recommend delaying weaning until 6 months means that your baby's immune system is far more likely to be able to react normally to foods. It's really only in families with a history of allergies that you need to watch key foods such as peanuts.

READY-PREPARED BABY FOOD

If you are buying commercially produced baby food, the ranges normally go from 4 to 7 months and 7 months upwards. In fact, there's no nutritional reason why a baby of 6 months can't eat food labelled 7 months-plus (although the consistency may need adjusting). But don't think just because a baby food is labelled as containing all the necessary vitamins and minerals that it's better than anything you can make yourself. Your baby will gain so much more from eating your own diet, and you can avoid needless sugar and salt, additives and preservatives, as well as saving yourself a lot of money.

STEPPING UP THE TEXTURE

As your baby gets older, you want her to tolerate texture and do more chewing, so over the next few weeks you need to make purées thicker and eventually mash the food rather than purée it. Even

if she doesn't have any teeth yet (they can start popping through any time from 6 to 12 months), it's good for her mouth and speech muscles to have something more than soft baby rice to chomp on.

CUTLERY

Small babies can't easily use their tongues to begin with, so use a small, shallow plastic spoon that they can run their lips over.

HOW MUCH FOOD YOUR 6-MONTH-OLD NEEDS PER DAY

Start with just one solid feed a day; I think this is best at lunchtime. Realistically, your baby is only going to want to eat one or two teaspoons of food to begin with – a couple of little ice cube-sized portions of, say, a rice and vegetable purée. As your baby gets more used to eating solids she'll have three or four cubes, sometimes more (when this happens, try freezing food in small pots, or little plastic bags).

stage 2: from 7 to 9 months

When your baby is roughly 7 months old, she's probably ready to progress to more complicated textures and tastes. By the time she's 9 months old she should be strong enough to sit in her own chair, will have a few teeth and will be happy to chomp through some finger foods, such as pieces of raw fruit and pasta shapes.

MILK

At 7 months it's a good idea to start reducing the amount of milk feed she has, so that she's hungry when you give solid food. She needs 500–800ml/18–30fl oz per day of infant formula or breast milk until she's a year old. The nutrients in the milk provide a cushion while you're getting her to eat normal food. You can add milk to her food if you like, but if you give it to her in a bottle you can make it a time to cuddle.

WATER

Since your baby's milk consumption is reducing, and she's eating solids, you will need to give her more water. This must be cooled boiled water (see page 22 for information about types of water).

NEW FOODS

Once your baby is happy eating from a spoon, start to include some protein foods such as eggs (well cooked), cheese (see page 51), chicken, fish, even meat, lentils, split peas, beans, etc. in her diet.

You should offer a wide range of foods in order to give her a good variety of nutrients. Variety also helps in getting her used to eating different flavours.

TEXTURE

The texture you're after now is mashed or minced, not puréed, as your baby needs to start chewing. By the time she is 9 months you can cut small grapes in half, give her chopped up fruits such as plums and peaches, and try dried fruits such as Medjool dates and prunes – but be sure to remove the stones.

SAUCES

Sauces are good for babies of this age, especially a simple cheese or tomato sauce. As they progress through stage 2 – at 8–9 months – they can join in with dishes such as spaghetti bolognaise, chicken casserole or fish pie. See my recipes for cauliflower cheese (page 140), beef casserole (page 129), bolognaise sauce (page 130), chicken and tomato couscous (page 122), chicken with bay leaves (page 125) and fish pie (page 134). Just be sure to mince or mash the dish before you give it to her.

SOUPS

Blend the soups or, if your baby is ready to chew, leave them with bits in. Soups of all sorts can be a great stop-gap – make a big cauldron and keep it in the fridge for

a couple of days, or freeze in manageable portions (see recipes on pages 110–111). Soups can be a good way of getting your baby to eat a variety of foods, and you can sneak all sorts of things into a soup and make them disappear by blending! For older babies, why not add dumplings, diced bread or croutons?

HOW MUCH FOOD YOUR 7–9-MONTH-OLD NEEDS PER DAY

At 7 months, aim each day to give 2–3 servings of starchy foods (a serving could be, for example, 25g/1oz of cooked pasta) and 1 serving of protein-rich food (say a well-cooked egg, a quarter of a small fillet of white fish or breast of chicken, or a large tablespoon of minced meat in sauce). She'll tuck into anything from 1 to 4 tablespoons of food at each mealtime and you should be increasing this as she progresses through stage 2. You can serve the protein with the starch, say fish with potato, at lunch or teatime – see how your day works and how your baby seems to like it. Some babies get on better with a more varied protein and starch meal at lunchtime.

You can give her more than this if she's hungry, and there will be days when she'll be at either end of the spectrum. Veggies and fruits are extra to these amounts.

NEW FOODS YOUR BABY CAN EAT FROM 7 MONTHS AT-A-GLANCE

All of these should be puréed at first and then mashed when your baby is ready.

Breads and cereals
• cooked wheat, rye, oats, spelt, buckwheat, couscous etc.
• pasta

New fruits
Start with a little, as the following can give young babies an upset tummy.
• citrus fruits – lemons, oranges, grapefruits, tangerines, mandarins, etc.
• berries – strawberries, raspberries etc.
• kiwi fruit and pineapple
• dried fruit – a little at a time (cooked and puréed until they're 9 months), as it can have a laxative effect.

Dairy
• cheese (avoid blue cheese at first)
• yoghurt, butter and well-cooked eggs
• various milks in cooking (see page 55)

Pulses
• cooked lentils and beans

Nut products
These are fine from 7 months if you haven't got a high-allergy family (otherwise wait until they're 3 years). Whole or chopped nuts are only suitable from 5 years.

Meat, poultry and fish
These are also fine from 7 months but be sure they are well mashed and don't contain bits of skin, bone or gristle.

CHEESE

Many parents are put off dairy for fear of overloading their baby's small body with too much saturated fat, or worry that dairy can cause mucus, aggravate colds or make babies constipated, none of which has any hard evidence to support it.

Cheese, like all dairy products, can be a nutritious food for your baby from an early age, offering a valuable source of calcium, zinc, protein and energy. Yes, it's quite high in saturated animal fat, but as long as you don't overdo it, it's a great food for your baby.

Cheese can be introduced as soon as you progress from fruit and vegetable purées. One of the best cheeses to start babies on is ricotta, which is only one step up from milk – it's mild and creamy, which they love, and easily digested. See my home-made ricotta (page 108) and the suggestions (right) from my friend, cheese guru Patricia Michelson.

EGGS

Well-cooked eggs, which can be mashed into vegetables and rice, are fine. Egg-fried rice is a quick and simple family supper to which you can add chicken, vegetables – in fact almost any leftovers. Mashed-up omelette, frittata, scrambled eggs or eggy bread (as long as the egg is well cooked) are good too once your child can cope with the texture.

Since soft-boiled or raw eggs carry an increased risk of food poisoning bugs

GOOD CHEESE FOR BABIES

Parmesan

Babies need only a very small amount of this cheese before feeling satisfied. It makes a good tea with thin slices of apple or pear or a few raisins or halved deseeded grapes. If you're travelling, slices of Parmesan (with rice cakes, dried and fresh fruits, etc.) are a nourishing snack. Rest assured that the salty taste is not really salt, but the proteins that have broken down in the milk as it matures.

Cheddar

Try good-quality Cheddar, grated finely and mixed with mashed potato, parsnip or carrot.

Cornish Yarg, Wensleydale (young) and Cotherstone

These crumbly cheeses have a sweetness to them that young tastebuds are attracted to; they mix well with vegetables. Other 'sweet' cheeses you can use in this way include Asiago Pressato, Comte d'Estive and young Manchego.

Goat's and sheep's cheeses

Some babies find these more palatable (although there isn't much difference in the digestibility of the different cheeses). Try the harder goat's and sheep's milk cheeses. There are also good goat's and sheep's milk products, such as cream, butter and yoghurt.

Avoid blue cheeses

Avoid blue cheeses until your baby is 12 months old. The moulds used in making these cheeses are strong and can upset delicate stomachs.

such as salmonella, you should avoid giving babies home-made ice-cream, mayonnaise and anything with raw egg in it. For babies over 12 months, I do use raw eggs in ice-cream and mayonnaise because I only ever use eggs with the British Lion mark, which means the eggs have come from chickens vaccinated against salmonella. If I were eating out, though, I wouldn't risk it, as only about 85 per cent of our eggs in this country have the seal on them.

See my recipes for eggy bread with fruits (page 157), egg 'majonaise' (page 114) and potato, pea and courgette fritatta (page 146).

YOGHURT AND FROMAGE FRAIS
Fromage frais and yoghurt are great for your baby. But stick to the full-cream versions of them.

I don't go for low-fat yoghurts because children need the full-cream varieties until they are at least 3 years old. Also, low-fat versions can have a lot of sugar added to them. When your child is 2 years old, growing well, and eating a well-balanced diet, you can gradually introduce lower-fat versions, but stick with good old full-cream for now. (See my home-made frozen strawberry yoghurt, page 168.)

Soya yoghurt is of course fine for vegan kids, but make sure you choose a calcium-enriched one. Normal soya yoghurt usually contains only about 15mg of calcium per 100g, compared to the classic cow's milk yoghurt which hits the 160mg per 100g mark, and this can make a big calcium difference to a young child. See my section on nutrition and the vegetarian or vegan baby (pages 80-81).

YOGHURT AND ALLERGIES
Yoghurt may be OK for babies and toddlers who are intolerant of cow's milk, as the fermentation processes involved can make it more digestible. However, seek your doctor's advice if you're worried about trying it. And note that this only applies to milk intolerance, not allergy.

Greek yoghurt is usually made from sheep's milk, which can be good for children who can't tolerate cow's milk proteins. The proteins are quite similar, though, so this yoghurt may not suit all children with cow's milk protein issues (see page 206).

CHILDREN'S YOGHURTS AND FROMAGE FRAIS
I hate the way many yoghurts aimed at children contain hefty doses of unnecessary sugar, additives and preservatives. Check the label. I go for natural full-fat yoghurt (cow's, goat's or sheep's) or fromage frais and add my own fruits, a dollop of apple, pear or apricot purée, pure fruit spread, or (from 9 months) chopped dried fruits. I'm a fan of organic yoghurt, but some of the children's versions have as much as 12g of added sugar per 100g – which is shocking!

BREAD AND CEREALS

You can start to introduce gluten-containing foods such as bread and pasta, as well as those made from grains such as spelt, rye, oat, buckwheat and millet – mashed up of course – which means you can ditch the baby rice now. Breakfast can be porridge, mashed Weetabix, or soaked and mashed muesli (no whole or chopped nuts until they're 5, but you can add dried fruits and seeds, apart from sesame seeds – grind them down to make them easier to swallow). Soaked mueslis are delicious with apple purée, or even grated pear – if you think the larger oats may be too much for them to manage, whiz them in a liquidizer.

With cereal foods such as bread, pasta and rice, you can use wholegrain or white (wholegrain products should be introduced slowly and limited for under 12-month-olds; see my section on fibre, page 71). I'd use a combination of both – and once your baby is 12 months, you can step this up to one meal with white, the next with wholegrain. Look at spelt and buckwheat pastas.

A word of warning about baby rusks: some of them contain so much sugar that I would give them a wide berth. Babies don't need them – a rice cake or breadstick is a much better dry food to nibble on, or even a slice of toast or pitta bread.

FISH AND SHELLFISH

Both oily and white fish are great for babies. Some babies take to oily fish really easily, even though it's a little strong-flavoured. But give her no

QUICK FISHCAKES, ENOUGH FOR BOTH OF YOU

Suitable for 8 months plus

150g/5oz cooked mashed potato, cooled
150g/5oz skinless and boneless oily or
  white fish fillet (or tinned salmon or tuna)
a dash of olive oil
a small handful of finely chopped parsley
a squirt of fresh lemon juice
pinch of freshly ground black pepper
mixture of plain flour and oats
1 egg, lightly beaten
a little olive oil, for frying

1 In a bowl, mix the mashed potato with the fish, olive oil, parsley, lemon juice and black pepper.

2 Divide the mixture into two portions and shape each one into a fishcake on a surface dusted with a mixture of plain flour and oats.

3 Dip each fishcake in the beaten egg.

4 Heat the oil in a large frying pan over medium heat. Add the fishcake and fry for a few minutes. When the fishcake is golden-brown underneath, turn it over and cook until completely golden. Mash or finely chop, if necessary.

more than two portions of oily fish (salmon, fresh tuna, sardines, mackerel, etc.) a week. Avoid tinned tuna in brine. Sardines mashed on warm toast is a good food for all the family – and see my fish pâtés (page 135).

Fishcakes (see left) are an easy way to get babies and toddlers to eat fish. Make up some salmon fishcakes with potato (delicious with sweet potato and carrot) and I bet they'll love them. And see also cod with roasted tomatoes (page 131) and fish fingers (page 132).

Shellfish such as prawns are fine for the whole family as long as they're well cooked and mashed up until your baby is ready for a chopped-up texture.

RED MEAT
Red meat is a great source of iron – one of the most important minerals for your child during her rapid growth years. Some parents worry about red meat's reputation as being high in saturated fat and a major cause of heart disease, but this only applies to poor-quality, fatty meat. Some lean red meat (beef, lamb or pork) can be perfectly healthy for your baby – mince it to begin with. Pork and lamb are lower in iron than beef, but still very nutritious. See page my home-made burgers (page 128) and slow-cooked beef casserole (page 129).

GAME
Game, despite its reputation for being rich, can be a lean (as in hardly any excess fat) way to incorporate protein into your baby's diet. Fillet of venison is

MILK IN COOKING
Although you should wait until your baby is 12 months to introduce cow's milk as a drink, it can be used in cooking from 7 months, and with breakfast cereal later on in stage 2. You can also use goat's, sheep's, buffalo, rice, soya, and oat milks (and nut milks if there is no allergy issue, see page 206). Follow-on formula can be used if you like – but I don't see the point.

However, be aware of allergies and other issues. Rice milk can contain barley protein, which means gluten too, so you shouldn't use it if gluten allergy is a concern (see pages 207-208). The same applies to oat milk. Note that oat milk and rice milk don't contain as much fat, calcium, and vitamin D as dairy milks. (For soya, see pages 30-31.)

particularly low in fat and high in protein, as are guinea fowl and rabbit; pheasant is higher in fat than some other game birds but still good for babies; lean duck meat (without its skin) contains no more fat than lamb (but if it's eaten with its skin on, even if it's crispy, duck is very high in fat). Venison sausages, though, are high in iron but they are also high in salt so are unsuitable for babies and toddlers.

OFFAL
There's no reason why a baby of 7 months shouldn't eat puréed or minced liver, so

FROZEN FISH

I'm all for frozen fish; it has swum a long way from the days when it was an inferior option. Nowadays, fish is more likely to be frozen at sea straight after being caught, so it can actually be fresher than so-called fresh fish. Be sure to keep it cool on its journey from the supermarket to your freezer. You can even cook it from frozen, although I prefer to defrost it.

Not all frozen fish is great quality, though. Sometimes inferior pieces are blast-frozen, which can damage the fragile flesh. Avoid cheap fish (the more carefully the fish has been treated, the more expensive it will be) and don't buy anything with 'snow' in the packet – a sure sign that the product has been exposed to temperature fluctuations.

Frozen fish will dry out if kept in the freezer for too long – the less time it is frozen, the better. If in doubt, follow the manufacturer's instructions.

long as it's well cooked. Pig's liver is perhaps a little strong for babies, but chicken livers are cheap and they are packed full of protein and iron. I've included chicken livers in my bolognaise sauce on page 130 – but if offal isn't your or your baby's thing, you can easily leave them out.

PASTA

Minced pasta usually goes down a storm with babies, as it's soft and easy to eat, and for older babies it's fun to suck wiggly pieces of spaghetti or pasta shapes. You don't need special alphabet pasta shapes or anything like that – just use the pasta you cook for the rest of the family. There are many types, from egg pasta to buckwheat. Spelt and rice pastas (try the thin transparent rice noodles) with a little vegetable or meat sauce make a quick nutritious meal for all. Wholegrain pasta provides some useful fibre, but babies under 12 months find it hard to cope with wholegrains so avoid or limit it until she is 1 year old.

COUSCOUS

Couscous is a quick and easy starch food (see my chicken and tomato couscous, page 122).

RICE

Rice (bar the ready-made processed packs with sauces) is good for everyone – from basmati to wild rice, Thai fragrant rice (aka jasmine rice), risotto or pudding rice. It's a great storecupboard staple and ideal for this stage of your child's eating plan so long as it's served in a texture she can cope with.

We tend to use only the common or garden white rice or risotto rice most of the time, but there are other great varieties, available in some supermarkets and delis. Try Carmague red rice (great in rice salads for older babies) or Nanjing black rice, which looks fun on a plate.

Nanjing rice is unmilled, so technically it's a wholegrain rice – which means you shouldn't give babies very much of it. It has a smoky flavour and works well with bright colours (babies can get bored with whiteness – as can we all!).

If you don't have any risotto rice (such as Arborio) you can use pudding rice for risotto. Equally, Arborio makes a great rice pudding. See my basic risotto and rice pudding recipes (pages 145 and 160).

LENTILS AND BEANS

Lentils, split peas and beans are all great at this age. And once they are ready for some texture, babies love playing around with beans in a sauce or tucking into beanburgers or falafel (see my recipes for bean crumble, page 137, falafel burgers, page 144, and simple daal, page 148.) Simply mush them up for 7-8 month-old babies if they are ready for the texture.

Hummus (home-made or bought – but check the salt level) is another winner, and is a good source of protein for vegetarians. I think hummus is good with virtually anything: once your baby can cope with finger foods (at around 9 months) put it on a plate for her to dip pieces of raw vegetable, toast, rice cakes, and pasta shapes into; spoon it over mushed jacket potatoes or use it to add some protein to a veggie rice dish. It's also good stirred into soups, which are ideal for 7-month-old babies.

NUT BUTTERS

These are fine for babies who don't have a family history of allergic diseases (see page 208). Use an unsalted smooth version, or make your own. As well as peanut butter, you can buy or make cashew, almond and hazelnut butters.

DRIED FRUITS

These are a great source of fibre, with a little iron and energy thrown in. Figs and prunes can have quite a strong laxative effect, which can be useful if your baby gets a little constipated (see page 199). Be sure to purée them for babies of this age – although by the time your baby is 9 months she may be able to eat dried fruit as a finger food.

I prefer to use fruits dried without sulphur dioxide (SO_2), as this can trigger asthma and tummy problems in some sensitive babies. Sulphur dioxide is used to preserve the brighter colours, and unsulphured fruits such as apricots are much darker. They vary a lot – some are tough as old boots while others are yummy – so shop around. Only give your baby a little dried fruit at a time, as they're sweet, sticky and too much can cause tummy-ache.

Meals should be more adult now. You can step up the texture again – food should be chopped or minced and some babies will cope with harder finger foods now – so your baby is having to work harder (although fruit purée and yoghurt is fine as a pudding). There should be little adaptation from the family's meals now – you just need to be careful about choking and avoid some foods, notably soft eggs, caffeine, salt and honey, and anything with a texture she can't cope with, for instance whole or chopped nuts.

Your baby wants to feel she's taking part in the same things as you, so sit and eat with her as much as possible from now on. If you find she's not eating from her own plate or bowl, pop some things on to your plate and allow her to take them off and mimic what you do – it's a small trick but it often works.

DON'T OVERDOSE ON MILK

A common mistake at this stage is to give babies too much breast milk or formula, which means they don't have enough of an appetite for solid food. Stick to 600ml/20fl oz per day (it's enough for first thing in the morning cuddles and last thing before bed at night). This will leave lots of room for eating food, which is what they love at this age.

WATER

You will need to give your baby more water now. Tap water is fine and it doesn't need to be boiled now as your baby's immune system is mature enough to deal with it straight from the tap.

HOMEMADE JUICES AND SMOOTHIES

The other great way to get some fluid, as well as some vitamins and minerals, into your baby is to make your own vegetable or fruit juices using a juicer. Drop the bottle other than at milk time – she needs to start using a tippy cup. You can also make smoothies (see page 158), but you'll need to dilute them with plenty of water so that they'll flow easily from your baby's cup.

NEW FOODS YOUR BABY CAN EAT FROM 10 MONTHS AT-A-GLANCE

a little more wholegrain

a little more oily fish

harder finger foods

NEW FOODS YOUR BABY CAN EAT FROM 12 MONTHS AT-A-GLANCE

softer eggs (e.g. scrambled eggs)

whole cow's milk and other milks (such as goat's, sheep's, soya, oat, rice) as a main drink

honey

HOW MUCH FOOD YOUR 10–12-MONTH-OLD NEEDS PER DAY

Give your baby two to three meals a day, with a couple of snacks such as fruit or rice cakes. You still need to include 500–600ml/18–20fl oz of breast milk or formula to top up her calcium and protein. Each day aim to give her:

• Three or four servings of starchy foods, such as bread, pasta, potatoes or rice. This can be breakfast, lunch and tea, with maybe a little rice cake snack in between. A serving is about 40g of cooked pasta (wheat, buckwheat, rice, spelt, etc.), which is about 15–20g of dry, and similar quantities for the other starches.

• One serving of animal protein or two servings of vegetable protein. Keep it unprocessed – don't go for sausages, for instance, unless you know they contain no salt. Similarly, cured meats, ready-made pâtés, salamis, etc. can be far too high in salt for babies. Animal protein foods include meat (lean red meat is good), fish (white and oily) and eggs (well-cooked). Vegetable protein foods include pulses (lentils, peas, beans) or nut butters (as long as there are no allergies in the family). 30g of cooked protein makes a portion.

• One or two servings of cheese, fromage frais or yoghurt (natural, full-fat).

These are only rough quantities – let your baby guide you. Some days she will eat more than these quantities, other days you'll be pushed to get her to eat half.

SELF-FEEDING

You will need plenty of patience when your baby's this age (well, actually, most ages if I'm honest). Mealtimes can be testing and tiring. But when you have a run of good days it makes up for all the bad ones (see fussy eating, page 95).

Usually by this age babies love to feed themselves, and can refuse if you try to take over. Hands will get into the food big-time, so it's one of the messiest stages – cover the floor, and get a Pelican bib that catches things! Babies love dipping things, so pieces of toast with soup, cucumber with hummus, and other finger foods go down well at this stage.

However, persevere with trying to get her to use a spoon, as it helps develop her fine motor skills and co-ordination. Most of the food will probably land on the floor, but the more she can experiment and have fun, the quicker she'll be able to feed herself. Parents who insist on feeding their babies are far more likely to end up with difficult eaters. Don't clean their fingers or wipe every drip as soon as they've made it – let food be fun; otherwise they might start using 'getting messy' as a controlling game.

Of course, extreme messiness isn't the answer either, but there should be a balance between seeing they are reasonably clean and being relaxed enough to let babies be babies.

CHOKING

Don't leave your baby on her own while eating, as she can easily choke at this stage. Do not give her whole or chopped nuts until she's 5. Remove seeds from grapes and cut them in half – especially the small ones, as they're perfect choking size. The same applies to anything with stones. Take chicken and meat off the bones. Also be careful with fish, as there are often little bones hiding. Don't let all this put you off; you just need to take care.

NEW FOODS

Now your baby's 10 months, you can really start widening her eating repertoire. She can tuck into lots of family foods, and will be happier to eat garlic, spices and more grown-up sauces, as long as they don't have salt in them.

Babies are usually at their most courageous and explorative now, so it's a good idea to try out different foods most days. If you keep giving your baby the same food, she can get fed up and refuse to eat it full-stop. It's a chance to get ahead before she gets older and starts being fussier. Always try foods a good 10 or 12 times before putting them to one side as something she may eat later. Of course there will be times when your baby spits things out and refuses to eat them, but be patient and try again a few minutes later. You shouldn't ever force her to eat something, but even if she just get a little taste in her mouth she will have been introduced to the flavours and it won't be as alien next time.

GOOD FROZEN BASICS

Having a good stock of basics such as risotto (see page 145) or veggie/tomato sauce (see pages 148-149) in the freezer will enable you to make different family meals with as little effort as possible.

SAVOURY VERSUS SWEET

It's important to persist with savoury meals and not to think, 'Well, they don't like that so I'll give them something fruity and sweet so that at least they have something inside their tummy.' Savouries should be what she eats most of the time and occasionally she'll get something sweet afterwards. The exception is when she's not well – on these occasions a little fruit purée or something that's guaranteed to be accepted will just tide her over.

'You shouldn't ever force her to eat something, but even if she just get a little taste in her mouth she will have been introduced to the flavours and it won't be as alien next time.'

IRON-RICH FOODS

Your baby needs more iron (an essential growth mineral) at this stage. Red meat is a great source but chewing it may be too much for your baby. I'd stick to good-quality minced beef, pork or lamb (which, although great, don't contain as much iron as beef). Either buy it ready minced (but choose good-quality, either 5 per cent or maximum 10 per cent fat) or make your own in a mincer. If you're having a steak for your own meal, cut off a piece and mince it for your baby. Other good iron-rich foods include eggs, beans, oily fish, dried fruits, broccoli and spinach.

DIRT

We live in an obsessive society when it comes to cleaning, and our dislike of dirt is not helping our babies to develop an appropriate level of immunity. Although the evidence isn't conclusive, it does seem that if babies over 6 months are not exposed to a minimum level of dirt and bugs (and similarly certain foods, especially ground peanuts and peanut products, unless they come from a family with a history of allergies), their immune systems can't develop an acceptable way to react to things in the environment. I don't mean let them pick food up off the floor, I simply mean you don't need to be extremely zealous with cleaning fluids. Babies can become over-reactive and develop conditions such as asthma, other types of allergies and diseases such as diabetes. In short, as well as being weaned at 6 months, challenged with lots of different foods, etc., our kids need to be allowed to be reasonably dirty – it's part of growing up and an important part of their development.

TODDLERS

When your baby is 12 months old, it's time to move on to the toddler stage. By now there should be very little she can't eat!

'If babies over 6 months are not exposed to a minimum level of dirt and bugs, their immune systems can't develop an acceptable way to react to things in the environment.'

equipment

CONTAINERS

Stock up with airtight plastic containers of all sizes. You need the very tiny ones that you can fit just a little leftover vegetable purée into and the larger ones which can store a batch of muffins or cakes. I've found small Tupperware pots great for making up yoghurts – you can pop in a few spoonfuls from a larger pot of natural yoghurt with some puréed or chopped dried or fresh fruit.

Get some greaseproof/baking paper to put between layers of cakes so that they freeze separately. And plastic ice-cube trays are invaluable for freezing foods such as purées, soups and risotto in small portions.

If you're short on freezer space, you'll find plastic bags are a good option, as more bags can be crammed into a smaller amount of space.

Remember to label bags or containers clearly – there's nothing more frustrating than defrosting something and then finding out it's not what you thought it was! Write the date as well as the name of the food on the label, as it's important not to leave things longer than the freezer manufacturer recommends.

BLENDERS AND LIQUIDIZERS

The one piece of equipment I've found invaluable as a mum is a hand-held

Plastic feeding equipment is essential – and a 'stick' blender is invaluable.

PREPARATION AND FEEDING KIT
- Shallow plastic feeding spoons
- Later, kids' cutlery
- Plastic bowls and plates
- Feeding cups with a spout and two handles
- Plastic bib with trough
- Plastic sheet for under the chair (optional)
- Hand-held blender
- Liquidizer (optional)

blender. You can simply pop it into a saucepan and make mash, soups, and fruit purées with very little effort – and it sure saves on the washing-up. They cost about £20–30, but will prove a worthwhile investment.

A liquidizer is useful for grinding up porridge oats or cereals, and making breadcrumbs to coat fish fingers. You can use it to turn a leftover casserole into a delicious soup (needing only croutons or a dollop of yoghurt to finish it), and if you're having a family meal of meat or chicken you can make it into a delicious purée for your baby.

CUPS, PLATES AND CUTLERY

Babies aren't able to take food off a deep metal spoon. Shallow, plastic feeding spoons are best to begin with, as they're unlikely to cause an injury. You can progress to kids' cutlery as your baby gets older.

Bowls with a suction pad are useful – and they reduce the amount of picking up you will need to do. And talking of picking up, a plastic sheet to put under the feeding chair is invaluable – it saves mess and also means you can pick things up and give them back to her.

Cups with a spout and two handles are great for first drinking. Finally, don't forget to get a plastic bib, with a trough to catch the food.

'A liquidizer is useful for grinding up porridge oats or cereals, and making breadcrumbs to coat fish fingers.'

APPROXIMATE LENGTH OF TIME YOU CAN STORE FOOD AT -18°C (0°F)

FOOD	MONTHS
Fruits and vegetables	8–12
Poultry	6–9
Fish	3–6
Meat	3–4

You need to be mindful of food hygiene. I am not suggesting that you become cleaning-obsessed, as exposure to germs is a vital part of the development of your child's immune system (see pages 61–62), but when it comes to food spoilage you need to be careful. Food poisoning in a baby or toddler can lead to dehydration and may be serious. And if you're tired and run down, you are more likely to fall victim to a food poisoning bug yourself.

ORGANIZING YOUR FRIDGE

Check that you're storing food properly in the fridge – see the manufacturer's instructions. Raw meat, for example, should be at the bottom of the fridge so that it can't drip over the other foods.

Wrapping refrigerated food well will prevent it from being contaminated by other foods in the fridge (for example, by drips from raw meat above it). Of course, it will also help keep it fresh for as long as possible. You can save a lot of money by keeping food well protected and this saving can mount up.

BREAD AND DRY GOODS

Like many other foods, bread and dry goods (such as crackers) will stay crisp in the fridge if you keep them well wrapped and/or in airtight containers.

Good labelling of frozen food is essential – write on the name and date of freezing.

STORAGE KIT
- Airtight plastic containers of all sizes
- Plastic freezer bags
- Freezer labels
- Greaseproof paper
- Plastic ice-cube trays
- Clingfilm

weaning and baby nutrition

Even though to begin with you will only give your baby a little food, keep in mind that his diet should be structured around the basic food groups. From 7 months you need to provide a balance of carbohydrates, proteins and fats in his solids. This way he can grow well, feel well, have enough energy and develop a strong immune system.

Like adults, every day he will benefit from a good variety of foods from each of the key groups shown opposite. He's in an active, growing phase, and his body needs to cope with the demands of growth and to start laying down good foundations.

The two biggest food groups he needs are starchy carbohydrates (bread, cereals, rice, and pasta) and fruit and vegetables. The next two groups are milk and dairy foods (yoghurt and cheese), and meat, fish and other protein foods (red and white meat, fish and shellfish, soya beans and tofu, nuts and seeds, pulses, lentils and grains). The smallest group is foods containing fat and sugar – these can be included from time to time as treats.

food wheel

starchy
carbohydrates

fruit and
vegetables

fish, meat, and
protein foods

milk and dairy
products

foods containing
fat and sugar

carbohydrates

Carbohydrates are the best source of the energy your baby needs to grow, so they should form the largest part of his diet.

COMPLEX CARBOHYDRATES

Complex carbohydrates include starchy foods such as bread, rice, pasta (white and wholegrain varieties) and potatoes, as well as some fruit and vegetables. They are a good source of many important nutrients as well as fibre (which even refined starchy foods provide, although not as much as unrefined versions) and they are also a rich source of energy. However, babies under 12 months can't cope with a lot of the bulky fibre found in wholewheat and bran, so foods made from these – for instance, wholemeal bread, brown rice and wholemeal pasta should be limited until your baby is 12 months.

SIMPLE CARBOHYDRATES

Simple carbohydrates include sugars that occur naturally in some foods (such as lactose in milk and fructose in fruit) as well as processed sugars, which are often referred to as added sugar. Naturally occurring milk and fruit sugars do not need to be avoided – they are an intrinsic part of healthy foods. But foods that contain added sugars (such as cakes,

COMPLEX CARBOHYDRATE FOODS

From 6 months
- puréed potatoes and root vegetables
- puréed sweetcorn
- puréed bananas

From 7 months
- puréed or mashed chickpeas
- ground nuts
- cooked porridge oats

From 8–9 months
- wholemeal breads and cornbread (soaked in milk and mashed if necessary)
- unsweetened muesli (powdered)
- brown rice, buckwheat noodles, spelt and barley (mashed or finely chopped)

SIMPLE CARBOHYDRATE FOODS

From 6 months
- baby rice

From 8–9 months
- white breads (soaked in milk and mashed if necessary)
- white pasta (mashed or finely chopped)

biscuits, sweets, and soft drinks) should be limited. They usually have little nutritional value and, unlike foods that contain complex carbohydrates, contain little or no fibre and so do not make us feel full, which makes it easy to overeat.

However, if your baby or toddler refuses to eat anything but white bread, don't worry; manufacturers legally must fortify white flour with thiamin, niacin, iron and calcium to put back some of the nutrients that have been removed.

A GOOD CARBOHYDRATE BALANCE

You should focus on fruit and vegetables up to 7 months. Wheat products can be introduced at roughly 8–9 months, but only give him the odd bit of wholemeal before he is 12 months.

In most cases, give children over 12 months roughly two-thirds white pasta, white bread, white rice to one-third wholemeal bread, wholemeal pasta, or brown rice. But do consider how well your child is growing, what his gut health is like (too much fibre can upset his gut, preventing him from getting enough energy from his food), whether he gets constipated, and if he is over-eating. I'd avoid highly refined, sweet, overly processed cakes and biscuits – homemade cakes such as walnut, fig or apple cake are better!

FIBRE

Not eating enough fibre can lead to constipation and even contribute to obesity, as fibre makes your child feel full. Fibre helps keep the digestive system working well and the heart healthy. It also helps the body balance blood sugar levels by slowing down the digestion and absorption of food (and this has an effect on your baby's energy levels and ability to concentrate and learn), and reduces the chance of him developing conditions such as diabetes.

Fibre can be soluble or insoluble. Soluble fibre is found mainly in fruits, vegetables and grains. Insoluble fibre is found in wholemeal foods. Babies and toddlers need both, but limit foods made from wholegrains until your baby is 12 months as young babies can't cope with too much fibre. Babies under 12 months should get their fibre mainly from peas, fruits and vegetable juices.

After 12 months, keep the peel on fruits such as apples and pears and include more wholegrain products, such as porridge or wholemeal bread. Avoid adding fibre in the form of bran or supplements unless prescribed by your doctor. Raw bran inhibits the absorption of essential growth minerals, such as iron and calcium, so should not be used.

fruit and vegetables

By the time your baby gets to 7 months he should be eating plenty of fruit and vegetable purées. Vary the vegetables as much as possible, because some are particularly rich in certain minerals and vitamins (carrots and beetroots are rich in beta-carotene, for example).

Tinned, frozen, cooked, and dried fruits and vegetables can be just as nutritious as fresh ones. (They may contain a little less vitamin C, but some manufacturers add it in supplement form.) Fruits and vegetables are frozen soon after they have been picked, which means they are just as healthy as fresh.

Buy tinned fruits in natural fruit juice, not sugary syrup. It's important to purée dried fruits until your baby is 9 months, as there is a choking risk, and only give a little at a time as they are very sweet and have a laxative effect.

By the age of 3 years, he will need three or four portions of fruit and vegetables a day. When your child is 2 or 3 he can explore whole fruits – there's so much goodness just inside the peel. Just make sure he sits down while he eats, so he doesn't choke.

FRUIT AND VEGETABLES

From 6 months

- Most vegetables need cooking. You may like to mash stronger-tasting vegetables, such as broccoli, green beans and peas, into some potato or sweet potato, or of course baby rice or oats.
- Most fruits need cooking. A few should be avoided (see 'From 7 months' below).
- Fruits and vegetables that don't need cooking (so long as they don't play havoc with his digestive system) are: cucumber, avocado, melon, soft peaches, plums, figs and bananas.
- Cooked chickpeas, potatoes, sweetcorn and root vegetables are a good source of natural starch.
- Shop-bought frozen vegetables and fruits are not only nutritious but can make your life much easier. Just steam or microwave a few frozen vegetables and blend them to whatever consistency your baby likes.

From 7 months

- Slowly introduce citrus fruits, berries, pineapple and kiwi, mashed.

From 8 months

- Pieces of ripe, soft peeled fruit make good finger fruits once he is ready to chew.

From 2–3 years

- Try giving him whole unpeeled fruits.

proteins

Your baby needs some protein every day for normal growth and development. Proteins provide amino acids, which are the building blocks of body cells and hormones. There are 22 amino acids, eight of which are called 'essential' because we can't make them in our body and so must get them from food. But too much protein can cause a child's kidneys to be over-burdened and may also compromise their bone health. Proteins are divided into two groups: animal-based and plant-based.

ANIMAL-BASED PROTEINS

Animal-based proteins contain good amounts of all eight essential amino acids (but you can also be healthy if you're vegetarian – see page 80). Young babies get all their animal proteins from milk.

PLANT-BASED PROTEINS

Plant proteins don't contain enough of the essential amino acids, so if they are to be a source of these essentials you need to give your baby or toddler combinations of plant protein foods, such as ground nuts and seeds (assuming there is no family history of allergies) and grains. Soya protein is the exception.

Although nuts and nut butters are great sources of protein, avoid peanuts until he's 3 years if you have a family history of allergies. And all children need to stay away from whole nuts until they're 5 because of the risk of choking.

PROTEIN FOODS

Animal-based proteins

From birth
• breast or formula milk

From 7 months
The following should be cooked and puréed or mashed where necessary
• yoghurt, eggs and cheese
• fish, chicken and meat

Vegetable-based proteins

From 7 months
The following should be cooked and puréed or mashed where necessary
• lentils, split peas and green peas
• chickpeas, butterbeans, kidney beans, borlotti beans and haricot beans
• ground nuts and seeds
• soya products
• cereal grains

fats

Babies need fats for brain function (to help them learn, behave, and concentrate), to keep them warm, to produce essential hormones for growth and development, and to ensure good absorption of vitamins. Of course they shouldn't have too much fat, but this does not mean they should tuck into low-fat foods, which can be high in sugar.

OMEGA-3S

We've all heard about 'good' fats and 'bad' fats. Omega-3 oils are good for brain function, hearts, joints, and virtually every part of the body. Introduce a little oily fish paté from 7 months; there is no reason why babies shouldn't like oily fish from an early age (a good friend's 8-month-old used to devour rollmop herrings by the shoal!).

By the time your toddler is 3 years, girls should have a couple of 80g/3oz portions of oily fish each week (they should not eat more, as there are concerns over the build-up of toxins in the body, which could harm babies born to them in the future); boys up to four portions (a maximum of two of which should be tuna, as there are concerns over mercury levels).

OTHER FATS

Fats from dairy produce, such as butter, cheese, cream, yoghurt and milk, are fine for babies as they contribute vitamins A and D.

OMEGA-3 FOODS

From 7 months
• mackerel, sardines, herrings, salmon, fresh tuna – mashed or patés are good
• oils such as hemp, walnut and flax (linseed)
• ground walnuts
• ground seeds such as sunflower and pumpkin (even for toddlers they are best ground up, as this aids absorption – I use the ground seeds in porridge, smoothies or cereal)
• nut butters too (assuming there is no family history of allergies) are rich in monounsaturated fats, one of the healthiest fats for us to eat. Check out cashew nut, hazelnut, and other butters (but remember, smooth varieties only)

To begin with your baby will only get small amounts of vitamins and minerals from solids, but breast milk or formula will provide a cushion. A good variety of fresh foods will give him enough vitamins and minerals to keep him healthy. One of the most important minerals is iron, and a key reason why we wean at 6 months is because breast milk and formula don't contain enough of this.

Vitamin A/beta-carotene: For healthy growth of body tissues, including skin; also protects against infection. Good sources are cantaloupe melon, peaches, pumpkin, squash, carrots, broccoli and courgettes. From 7 months try well-cooked egg yolk, cheese and mackerel.

Vitamin D: For strong, healthy bones and teeth. It is mainly manufactured by the skin when exposed to sunlight, but other good sources from 7 months are: sardines, herrings, salmon, tuna, cheese, well-cooked eggs and yoghurt. Margarines are fortified by law.

Vitamin E: An antioxidant, important for the heart, blood, skin, and immune system. Good sources are avocados, broccoli and spinach. From 7 months try vegetable oils, ground almonds, ground sunflower seeds and well-cooked eggs.

Vitamin K: Essential for helping blood to clot (babies are given an injection of it

after birth). You need to top up supplies as they grow. Good sources from 7 months are bio-yoghurt, well-cooked egg yolks, fish oils, dairy and green leafy vegetables.

Vitamin B$_1$: For energy, digestion, the heart and nervous system. A good source is potatoes; from 7 months, oats and liver.

Vitamin B$_2$: For energy and for normal structure and function of membranes and skin. A good source is green leafy vegetables; from 7 months, bio-yoghurt, milk (as an ingredient), and cottage cheese.

Niacin: For energy, the skin and the nervous system. Found in most foods, but meat is the major source.

Pantothenic acid: For conversion of fats and carbohydrates into energy and for supporting the adrenal glands, which regulate the stress response in the body. Get it from green leafy vegetables such as spinach; from 7 months, chicken, ground nuts and egg yolks; from 12 months, wholegrains, rye, barley, millet.

Vitamin B$_6$: For protein metabolism. Sources from 7 months are chicken, turkey, lean red meat, well-cooked egg yolks, oily fish, dairy produce, cabbage and leeks; from 12 months, wheatgerm.

Vitamin B$_{12}$: For cell division (growth) and blood function. From 7 months, get it from red meats, fish, well-cooked eggs, and dairy produce.

Folate: For the growth of body tissues and formation of blood cells. Good sources are dark green leafy vegetables, carrots, apricots, melons (particularly cantaloupe), squash and orange juice. From 7 months, well-cooked egg yolks; from 12 months, wholewheat and rye.

Biotin: For hair, nails, skin, and energy. Found in fruits. From 7 months in nuts (as nut oils/butters, or ground), well-cooked egg yolks; from 12 months brown rice.

Vitamin C: For a good immune system, a healthy heart, good skin, and helping cuts to heal. Best sources are berries, pomegranate juice, potatoes, squash, sweet peppers, green leafy vegetables, broccoli, cauliflower and spinach. From 7 months, citrus fruits and kiwi fruits.

MINERALS

Calcium: For bones and teeth, and muscle function. Found in green leafy vegetables; from 7 months, in dairy, soya products, almonds (ground), sesame seeds (ground or in tahini/hummus), sunflower seeds (ground), and dried fruits (puréed).

Iron: For growth and development and the production of healthy red blood cells. One of the main reasons why solids are introduced at 6 months. Get it from peaches, apricots, figs, asparagus, bananas, spinach, watercress, broccoli, avocados, and fresh herbs; from 7 months, from lean red meat, nuts (ground), prunes (puréed), lentils, sunflower seeds (ground) and well-cooked egg yolks; from 12 months, beans in tomato sauce, oatmeal, fortified breakfast cereals, wholemeal bread and brown rice.

Magnesium: Helps the body deal with stress, generate energy and build strong, healthy bones; also helps with muscle function and the nervous system. Found in green vegetables such as broccoli, carrots, potatoes, aubergine, and sweetcorn; from 7 months, nuts and seeds (ground), dried fruits (puréed) and tomatoes.

Selenium: For the immune system. In all fresh fruit and vegetables; from 7 months, in sesame seeds and brazil nuts (ground); from 12 months in wheatgerm.

Zinc: For the immune system, sexual development, moods, the nervous system and brain function. Sources include cauliflower and berries; from 7 months, fish, lean red meats, chicken, turkey, nuts and seeds (ground), well-cooked eggs, dairy and oats; from 12 months, rye, wheatgerm, brown rice, spelt and buckwheat.

organic foods

I believe organic food is best for babies in most cases. It is regulated to control the use of pesticides and hormones, and organic farmers work to make the food as tasty as possible. local matters too. Local organic food is seasonal, and it's good for kids to appreciate the seasons.

It's also worth remembering that some non-organic farms are working hard to minimize the use of pesticides – they simply might not have the high organic standards necessary for certification. This doesn't mean their produce is bad. I would buy local non-organic food, but I'd ask questions about its quality first.

And remember, organic junk food can mount up the calories or rot the teeth. Just because a crisp is made from organic potatoes doesn't mean it's healthy.

THE COST OF ORGANIC

Organic food doesn't come cheap. My solution is to eat the pricey items such as meat less often and use cheaper organic ingredients such as pulses to make meat go further. But if you can't afford organic, don't feel bad; just try to buy as much fresh produce as possible and wash it well.

MEAT

Animals are more likely to be kept in poor conditions and given antibiotics in non-organic farms. But there are farmers producing good meat without organic certification; they may have missed out on certification simply because they have trouble getting hold of organically certified feed. For a directory of organic butchers, see www.organicbutchers.co.uk.

FISH

The question of organic is not so simple with fish. Organic fish is pricey and hard to find, plus it's usually farmed, which I have an issue with on environmental grounds. I support the Marine Conservation Society's (MCS) campaign to protect our over-fished species by only buying fish from protected waters. The MCS has produced a list of the 20 species of fish to avoid and the 25 species you can eat with a clearer conscience. See www.mcsuk.org.

EGGS AND MILK

The Food Standards Agency assures us that the levels of hormones fed to cattle are safe, but I still prefer to buy organic milk and/or milk from a good local supplier. If you can't get organic eggs, try free-range. Ensure they have the British Lion mark (showing the chickens have been vaccinated against salmonella).

FRUIT AND VEGETABLES

Organic fruit and vegetables often don't look as attractive as non-organic, but don't let this put you off. It's good to bring up children to accept knobbly apples and non-spherical oranges.

Some parents decide to bring up their baby as a vegetarian for ethical reasons, others for perceived health benefits. Of course lots of poor, fatty meat and a lack of fruit and vegetables is unhealthy, but there's nothing wrong with a nutritious diet that includes good-quality meat, chicken and fish. From 7 months, a baby's digestive system is perfectly capable of dealing with red meat and other animal products, as long as you choose them well and incorporate them into your child's diet alongside other nutritious foods.

It is perfectly possible to bring up a happy, healthy little vegetarian. But a vegetarian diet is not inevitably healthy. You need to watch elements such as saturated animal fats (think of butter, cream, and cheese), hydrogenated fats (check processed food labels – even the pricey brands contain them), and sugars (drinks are major offenders).

BABIES WHO DON'T LIKE MEAT

It can take babies a while to get used to the texture of meat and fish, so don't give up just because they don't like it at first. Some suddenly start rejecting meat or fish as toddlers, but this doesn't mean they don't like it. All foods take some getting used to, and your baby or toddler is just as likely to start playing up with meat as he is with anything else. Before you stop giving meat to a toddler because you think he doesn't like it, try mincing it or incorporating it into everyday foods, for example finely chopped ham in mash potato.

BENEFITS OF A VEGETARIAN DIET

There are numerous benefits to a vegetarian diet. You baby is more likely to eat lots of fresh fruits and vegetables and there is evidence to show he is less likely to suffer as an adult from conditions such as obesity, bowel cancer and heart disease. But do ensure that your baby gets all the essential nutrients.

FIBRE

Fibre needs to be finely balanced in his diet. Too little can leave him constipated, too much can leave him anaemic and low in energy. Babies find it difficult to cope with bulky fibre (see page 71). A diet focused on vegetables can easily lead to too much fibre. If his weight doesn't increase as it should do or he's always tired he may be getting too much.

PROTEIN

The amino acids that protein foods contain are important for your baby. Every week a vegetarian baby needs a variety of different vegetable proteins, with some cereal added for babies over 12 months (see page 74).

A plentiful supply of five key minerals – calcium, magnesium, iron, zinc and selenium – is important (see page 77). It's much easier to ensure that babies take in enough minerals if they eat dairy produce, but there are a few non-animal sources of these minerals.

ENERGY

Energy sources for vegetarian babies can most usefully come from fats and carbohydrates (see pages 70, 71, and 75)

Dairy foods are great for energy (and a good source of calcium and vitamins). But too much dairy can lead to excessive weight gain, and too much saturated fat can lead to heart disease and some types of cancer in the future.

Ensure carbohydrate foods for your baby are the healthiest and least bulky – fruit purées and compotes are good.

Vegetable fats are found in avocados, nuts, seeds (hemp, pumpkin, sunflower, linseeds, sesame), coconut (milk, flesh, oil), olive oil, hemp oil, avocado oil, nut oils, and nut butters (avoid seeds and nuts if there is any family history of allergies). The fat tends to be mainly unsaturated, which is better for the heart (with the exception of coconut, which has a high saturated fat content). They can still, in excess, put too much weight on babies, but in moderation the fat can be good. I use a little coconut in cooking sometimes, but I wouldn't rely on coconut oil as a baby's main source of fat.

Soya and soya products tend to be low in fat, which means they're good for kids' hearts but not great for energy (see page 31). You need to add an alternative vegetable source of energy to their diet.

VEGAN WEANING

It's increasingly easy to wean a baby as a vegan, not that supermarkets stock soya and tofu, fortified soya milks and soya yoghurts. You need a good balance of fresh ingredients; processed foods such as tofu sausages can contain salts, preservatives, bad fats, and so on. There are lots of vegan recipes in this book.

Consult your doctor and/or a paediatric dietitian if you are considering weaning your baby as a vegan. You may need to discuss supplements. You particularly need to watch that your vegan baby gets enough vitamin B_{12}. You can buy fortified soya drinks, spirulina (a form of algae), low-salt yeast spreads (the full-blown ones are far too high in salt for kids) and fortified breakfast cereals (but check labels for sugar and salt), depending on the age of your baby.

My favourite vegan foods for babies over 7 months are: seed patés such as hummus and nut butters (assuming no family history of allergies), plus oils such as olive or hemp and avocados (suitable from 6 months).

FAT

You need to think a little about the type and amount of fat you feed him. Many parents think that we should avoid saturated animal fats and only consume foods made with vegetable fats. But it's all about balance.

Saturated fats produce LDL, the 'bad' cholesterol that can cause heart disease and other problems later. But dairy is fine within a balanced diet. And vegetable fats aren't always good. Olive and vegetable oils are OK in their raw state, but if they're used in spreads and cakes the food-manufacturing process will turn these good fats into bad.

SUGAR

As a new parent, you have the chance to establish a healthy pattern when it comes to sweet things. Babies should eat some sweet foods, but in the right amounts. If you can start your baby off on a naturally low-sugar diet, he won't miss the extreme sweetness of so many refined sweet foods (the same applies to salt).

Sugar provides calories – but they are empty calories, since it doesn't contain any other nutrients. Added sugars are not necessary in your baby's diet. There are many other names for added sugars (e.g. sucrose, glucose, fructose, corn syrup, etc.) so you need to look for it on food labels. Nutrition information on labels can be confusing when it comes to

DRINKS

Give your baby water rather than juice for as long as possible. (However, if your baby is vegetarian, a little diluted orange juice with meals will help with his iron absorption as iron is not absorbed as easily from vegetables as from meat.) If you do want to give juice occasionally, make sure it's well diluted (one part juice to 10 of water), give it in a trainer cup or beaker, not a bottle, and only give it at mealtimes; this will protect his emerging teeth.

the sugar content. If manufacturers provide nutrition information, they are legally obliged to state the total amount of sugar present. However, this total does not differentiate between sugars found naturally in an ingredient such as apple or milk and sugars that have been added as a separate ingredient, such as sucrose. What this means is that the total sugar content can sometimes seem much worse than it is. For example, in 100g/3½oz of yoghurt, about 4g/⅛oz of the total sugars is from lactose in the yoghurt itself; any additional sugars are likely to be added sugars, although they could be from a pure fruit purée. The only way to know is to check the list of ingredients and see how near the beginning any added sugars are listed – the main ingredients must be listed first.

Babies don't know that pudding is a classic follow-on to the savoury part of a meal, unless it always does. So I suggest that you do not give them a sweet course every time but maybe on alternate days.

NATURALLY SWEET FRUIT AND VEG

Fruit purées contain a range of nutrients (such as vitamins) and babies usually accept them willingly. Some vegetables are naturally sweet, in particular parsnips, swede, carrots, peas and sweet potatoes. You can mix fruits and vegetables – carrot purée with stewed apple, or mashed sweet potato with a few well-cooked lentils.

HONEY

Honey must not be given to babies under 12 months because it can occasionally cause infant botulism. But it has useful antiseptic properties and a higher water content than sugar, which means it has fewer calories and is less sweet. It's good to include it, in moderation, in your toddler's diet after the first year.

Good-quality honey has antibacterial properties – it can help heal wounds and mouth ulcers and it can soothe a sore throat – but bog-standard honey won't help combat infection. Choose an organic honey from bees that frequent only one flower, or the New Zealand Manuka honey (dark and strong, so not all kids may like it, but a medicine-cabinet must-have). Look for pure honeycomb too.

ACCEPTABLE SALT LEVELS

In the first 6 months of life, your baby needs less than 1g of salt per day, which he will get from breast milk or formula. Between 7 and 12 months this increases slightly, to around 1g. Toddlers aged 1–3 years old can have 2g. Salt is 40 per cent sodium; to work out how much salt something contains you need to multiply the sodium level by 2.5. So 1g (100mg) of sodium equals 2.5g of salt (2,500mg).

Scrutinize labels. Manufacturers sometimes don't have to declare how much salt is in a food, but check how far salt or sodium is in the list of ingredients – if it's near the top, there's quite a lot.

SALT LEVELS IN BABY FOOD

If you keep your child's dietary salt levels low when he's a baby, he won't miss it when he's older. Once your child is over 7 months, use flavourings such as lemon juice, pepper, garlic and fresh herbs. Foods made specifically for babies, such as those in jars and infant cereals, have a low salt content, since they're governed by strict legislation. But processed foods aimed at older children, such as crisps, can contain a lot of salt.

There will be times when your toddler tucks into crisps, and the occasional one is not going to harm him. Try the delicious no-salt vegetable varieties.

probiotics to heal

Everyone has 'friendly bacteria' in their gut, which help maintain a healthy digestive system. The gut also contains harmful bacteria such as E.coli and salmonella; this is natural and important to our immune systems. But too many bad bacteria can cause wind and tummy-ache.

WHAT PROBIOTICS DO

Probiotics help balance bacteria. Probiotic bacteria are introduced to a baby's diet through breast milk. Illness and antibiotics (which can kill good bacteria as well as bad) can upset the balance.

Research has found probiotics can help treat diarrhoea caused by antibiotics and tummy bugs. They may also prevent food poisoning, improve lactose intolerance symptoms, reduce susceptibility to dermatitis and help control irritable bowel symptoms. Trials also suggest probiotics can strengthen the immune system and reduce cholesterol levels. A daily dose of probiotic Lactobacillus rhamnosus bacteria given to pregnant women and to their babies during the first 6 months of life may reduce the incidence of eczema.

HOW TO GIVE A BABY PROBIOTICS

It's worth thinking about giving a baby over 6 months a probiotic for getting over short-term problems such as a tummy bug or if he's taking antibiotics. Give him a daily capsule of probiotic bacteria containing at least a billion bacteria per dose (they need to be kept in the fridge) for two weeks. Do not give whole capsules to children under 5 years. Instead, dissolve the capsule in cooled boiled water, add it to formula or sprinkle it into a smoothie. Keep probiotics away from anything hotter than hand-hold temperature, as heat kills the bacteria.

Make sure the capsules have been refrigerated in the shop, and check the labels to ensure they contain one or all of the following: Lactobacillus casei, Lactobacillus delbrueckii, Bifidobacterium adolescentis, Bifidobacterium longum, Bifidobacterium infantis. You can buy single strains, or a mix of the bacteria, and both are great. If your child is lactose-intolerant, check the label, as some supplements contain lactose. The drinks containing these bacteria are often high in sugar and colourings. Day-to-day I'd give a baby over 7 months a live natural yoghurt.

PREBIOTICS

It's good to help your baby produce and maintain his own good bacteria. Prebiotics are carbohydrates that feed the friendly bacteria. Foods rich in prebiotics are asparagus, bananas, garlic, leeks, milk (as an ingredient), onions, tomatoes and yoghurt. If your baby has a medical problem that requires a probiotic supplement, ask your doctor if he should take a probiotic that also has prebiotics, or a separate prebiotic supplement.

drinks

FRUIT JUICE

If you give your baby or toddler fruit juice, buy or make unsweetened pure juice, dilute it to at least three parts water to one of juice, and offer it just once a day. The maximum amount of juice per day for babies under 18 months is 200ml/7fl oz. Too much juice can cause indigestion, a bloated tummy, diarrhoea or constipation, and can pile on weight.

Juice can provide vitamin C but if you always offer it, it will damage your baby's teeth and give him the message that water is boring. Ready-made juices can be highly processed, sweetened, coloured and preserved.

Don't clean your baby's teeth straight after he has juice. The acid and sugar levels in his mouth at at their highest then, so you'll damage the teeth.

HOME-MADE JUICES

Home-made fruit smoothies and juices are good. But juicing removes most of the fibre from the fruit. Drinks made by putting the whole fruit into a blender keep more fibre. Also, because drinks are consumed more quickly than fruit, your baby's body can get more of a 'sugar hit'.

You can add vegetables to home-made fruit juices – carrots, fennel and celery to apple juice, for example. Juices should be drunk as soon as possible to get the maximum levels of vitamins.

READY-MADE JUICES

UHT juices in airtight cartons can contain as many vitamins and minerals as ready-made freshly squeezed ones. Pick one without preservatives, preferably organic, and only give them to 18-month-olds plus.

HOT DRINKS

It's fine for kids over two to have the occasional cup of very weak tea – it's a comforting antioxidant-packed drink and the milk is good for them. But keep it weak so they don't get the caffeine hit. Coffee has too much caffeine for them. Hot chocolate drinks can contain quite a lot of a caffeine-like substance called theobromine, as well as sugar, which could disrupt sleep. So only give it earlier in the day and choose a good-quality brand. Warm milk is a good drink for getting babies and toddlers to sleep well.

how to cook a baby's food

PREPARING FRUIT AND VEGETABLES

Prepare vegetables and fruits at the last minute. The longer cut and peeled surfaces are exposed to the air, the more nutrients will oxidize and disappear. Scrub them rather than peeling, as many nutrients are just under the skin

MICROWAVES

If you microwave vegetables, soluble nutrients don't leach out into the water as they do when vegetables are boiled. This is because the microwave cooks vegetables quickly and doesn't require much water.

There has been a lot of speculation in the press that microwaves are bad for our health, with scary words like 'irradiation' and 'carcinogenic' being bandied about. But don't be put off: microwaving is a very safe way to cook, as long as you follow the manufacturer's instructions.

STEAMING AND BOILING

To avoid loss of nutrients, I recommend steaming vegetables rather than boiling them. If you do boil them, you should keep the cooking time to a minimum.

SLOW COOKERS

Slow cookers are great: there's nothing like walking in at the end of a full day and finding a delicious, sweet-smelling casserole ready and waiting. There are many nutritional advantages to letting foods cook slowly. First, if you give ingredients time to simmer, mix and infuse, the natural flavours will develop and deepen – which enhances the flavour without the need for salt. Second, slow cooking ensures that vegetables and pulses such as beans and lentils are well cooked so they're relatively easy to digest. Third, slow cooking enables less confident cooks to use root vegetables such as celeriac, swede and parsnips, without having to worry about the exact timing – you just throw it all in and let the slow cooker do the work

Casseroles, spaghetti bolognaise and tagines (Moroccan one-pot cooking) all work particularly well in a slow cooker, and can all be puréed if necessary.

feeding
a toddler

A one-year-old's stomach simply isn't big enough to hold the amount of food she needs to keep her going until the next meal. So whilst it's good to get into the habit of giving her three good meals a day, you can incorporate a couple of nutritious snacks at regular times too. As she gets older these snacks can be phased out.

Snacks aside, there isn't a noticeable difference between the eating day of a 12-month-old and a 3-year-old. There will, of course, be small variations in quantities, preferences and likes and dislikes, but for ease I have treated the age ranges the same.

How much your toddler needs to eat depends on how active she is. Some children tend to be more hungry at lunchtime; others are happy with a lighter lunch and a more substantial tea. You can be guided by your child.

your toddler's eating day

There are only a couple of basic rules about your toddler's eating day. Firstly, in a day she should eat some foods from each of the four main food groups: starchy carbohydrates; fruit and vegetables; milk and dairy foods; and meat, fish and protein-rich foods. You don't need to have something from each group at every meal, but it's a good guide to base the day around.

Secondly, even toddlers as young as 12 months need to know that food comes at certain times – that they sit and eat it and then it's over. Try not to always give her a snack to pacify her; she may not really be hungry and all you're doing is getting her into the habit of being given far too much food. She may just be thirsty, so offer water first, a cuddle, or something different to play with.

COW'S MILK

At 12 months it's fine to switch from breast milk and formula to cow's milk – full cream, not semi-skimmed, as your toddler needs the extra fat for energy and growth. When she's 2 years old you can switch to semi-skimmed, but don't change to skimmed milk until she's 5 years old.

You can also use goat's, sheep's, rice or soya milk, but because their fat content – and indeed their nutrients – are different from full-cream cow's milk, you need to ensure that you make up the nutritional shortfall elsewhere.

FOODS TO AVOID AT 12 MONTHS

Whole nuts (and chopped nuts if there is any history of food allergies)

Unpasteurized cheese

Excessive salt

Excessive refined or unrefined sugar

Tea and coffee

'In a day your toddler should eat some foods from each of the four main food groups.'

breakfast

A good breakfast will help your toddler to concentrate, memorize things, solve problems, and be creative.

PORRIDGE

Porridge is a great stand-by, not least because you can add a lot of yummy ingredients to it. Add honey, fruit spread, date syrup, brown sugar, fructose powder (which has a lower GI value than cane sugar), or fresh, puréed, poached or dried fruits. With fructose (the sugar you find in fruit) you need less than you would need with ordinary white sugar to achieve a yummy sweet taste, and your toddler's energy levels should be more consistent. You can buy it from www.goodnessdirect.co.uk. In spring and summer try adding gooseberries, raspberries, strawberries, kiwi fruit or sliced oranges; in autumn and winter go for apples, blackberries, pears or plums. Finely chopped nuts and seeds can be good too.

EGGS

Eggs make a good protein-rich topping for toast. After 12 months your toddler can have a runny boiled egg, so toast soldiers can make an appearance. They can be scrambled or poached, and served with cooked mushrooms, sliced tomatoes – all the grown-up breakfast options can work for her. Just watch salty foods such as bacon and sausages, and try not to OD on smoked fish such as kippers.

BREAKFAST CEREALS

Some breakfast cereals are OK (lot's aren't though – too much salt, sugar, or saturated fat – see the *Which?* report on breakfast cereals at www.which.co.uk). Weetabix and Shredded Wheat are pretty good high-fibre options, as are the Sharpham Park spelt cereals and the Dorset range. The Peter Rabbit range of cereals is also great. Top with fruit if your toddler won't eat them plain – but don't pile them on.

CEREAL BARS

Most contain more sugar and fat than cakes and biscuits. So don't be fooled by the wholesome-looking packaging; most should be given a wide berth.

QUICK BREAKFAST IDEAS

There are so many things you can feed your toddler aside from shop-bought cereals (which often have a high salt content). Muesli can be a good option, especially if served with fresh fruits – just add a little full-fat milk, yoghurt or fromage frais. Other simple ideas include: yoghurt with stewed fruits and perhaps honey; fruit muffins; bagels or toast with fruit purée or banana; and fruit home-made fruit juices or smoothies.

---

lunch and dinner

What your toddler eats during the day will depend partly on whether she's at home or at the nursery.

SNACKS

There are times when your toddler will need a nutritious snack. Toddlers can burn through food quickly, and between-meal pit-stops can be a good way to get a few extra fresh fruits and vegetables into them. Some of my best pit-stops are grissini, rice cakes, oatcakes, dried fruits (unsulphured) and fresh fruits.

LUNCH

If your toddler has her main meal at lunchtime, it's important to keep her active in the morning so she can build up an appetite. After a larger lunch (especially one that includes starches such as pasta, rice and potatoes) she may feel more tired. If she has a light lunch, make sure it still contains some protein as well as carbohydrate. Chicken, meat, fish and eggs are all high in protein – but use good vegetarian sources too, such as beans, lentils, tofu and chopped nuts.

DINNER

Toddlers need a good meal at the end of the day, but try not to feed them too late. If your routine means you get home late – maybe driving her back from a childminder – try to make sure she's had a good big cooked lunch and a good mid-afternoon snack, so she only needs a small tea before bed. I'm not saying this is the best routine, but sometimes kids are too tired for anything else.

Jacket potatoes are great. Serve them with coleslaw, tuna mayonnaise or even baked beans (but check salt levels). In the summer, salads can go down well – toddlers love mini versions of things, so try baby tomatoes with butter beans and tuna.

Easy puddings include yoghurt with fruit and even some seeds. Toddlers love banana with yoghurt, and stewed fruit and fruit compotes are always popular.

READY MEALS

Whilst ready-made meals in jars and packets are not always bad, watch out for salt, sugar, preservatives and additives.

QUICK LUNCH AND DINNER IDEAS

For a lighter meal, try warm pitta bread with a homemade dip, such as avocado and cream cheese, or with cottage cheese.

For more substantial meals, pasta is always handy, and can be mixed with a quick tomato sauce or cheese and a vegetable such as sweetcorn or peas. Rice is equally useful, and quick rice dishes include rice with chicken and a vegetable such as green beans or rice with bacon and a vegetable such as peas.

fussy eaters

With all toddlers there are times when everything else seems far more exciting than food and they're just not interested in eating. Don't worry – on other days they'll eat so much that it will even out. Feast and famine is the norm. It can be alarming when your toddler goes for a few days without appearing to eat much, but it's normal and the opposite gear will soon kick in. (Of course, if you're worried or your child appears to be unwell, you should seek advice from your doctor.)

There will be times when your toddler is so keen on a specific food that she'll want to eat it constantly. Try not to give in too often – it can lead to power games, with a child asking for one thing, then refusing to eat it and asking for another.

EATING AS A FAMILY

Your one-year-old should be sitting down and eating the same nutritious foods as you. Her tastes can be sophisticated and, apart from whole nuts, unpasteurized

WON'T EAT VEG?

When it comes to vegetables, try to serve them in different guises – roasted, puréed or stuffed. As long as your child eats one or two types a day, she should get enough nutrients. If she's going through a really bad patch and won't touch vegetables at all, even when you disguise them in sauces, you could giving her a children's multivitamin and mineral supplement in the short-term. However, there's no substitute for real fresh food, so each week have a go at coaxing her back to the real thing (remember – she may need to try a food 10-12 times before she will happily eat it).

WON'T EAT FRUIT?

It's unlikely that you won't be able to find a fruit your toddler enjoys – from clementines, mangoes, figs and kiwis to pears, apples and bananas – because most toddlers appreciate their sweetness. If you do have a problem, blend fruits into a smoothie or freeze pure fruit purées to make ice-lollies or ice-creams, or purée, cook and stuff fruits to make them more appealing to your toddler.

Fruit smoothies are usually winners (use fresh fruits and add frozen berries to save time and money), especially if you can involve your toddler in choosing which fruits go in the blender and she can press the button (check the lid's on!). You should dilute the smoothie roughly 50:50 with water, to protect her tummy and teeth (acids can damage the enamel).

cheese, salt, sugar and caffeine, nothing's off the menu – you just need to watch for things such as stones as well as different textures. So your child can tuck into all the recipes in this book. Just watch that you're not expecting her to eat on her own too much, as toddlers are far more likely to eat well if they're with the whole family.

POWER GAMES

If your toddler is a fussy eater, try not to worry too much. Avoid slipping into waitress-style feeding – cooking children something else if they reject your first offering. Although this doesn't matter occasionally, never forget that toddlers will eat when they're hungry.

I'd also recommend that you step back from always fussing – kids cotton on to this and can dig their heels in even more. Keep a watchful eye from a distance.

ENCOURAGING YOUR CHILD TO EAT

If your child won't eat, enlist the help of stories and toys – try serving a meal for them too. This role play can be tiring, but it can really work. Tap into rewards, such as a trip to the playground. It's important to have non-food rewards.

Try to get your toddler to try something before she rejects it – even if it's only half a teaspoon. She may realize that it's nice after all. And try to stay as relaxed as is humanly possible!

If getting your child to be less fussy is a general problem, I suggest trying each new food 10 to 12 times, with days in between, before you give up on it. Blending and puréeing foods to disguise them in soups and pasta sauces, or putting carrots or parsnips in with the mashed potatoes, usually works too.

SHOP AND EAT TOGETHER

Finally, do as much as possible together – shop together, choose foods together, cook together and eat together. I can't emphasize enough how much good this can do. I know shopping with a toddler can be difficult, but if you're both feeling on edge, see if it can wait until tomorrow – supermarkets can be one of the most embarrassing places for screaming abdabs! When you can go shopping together, it helps build up your child's relationship with the food. Spend a few minutes talking about the foods you're putting in your trolley, so she learns the names and sees foods as fun. Let her help unpack a few items and help you put things away in the right place.

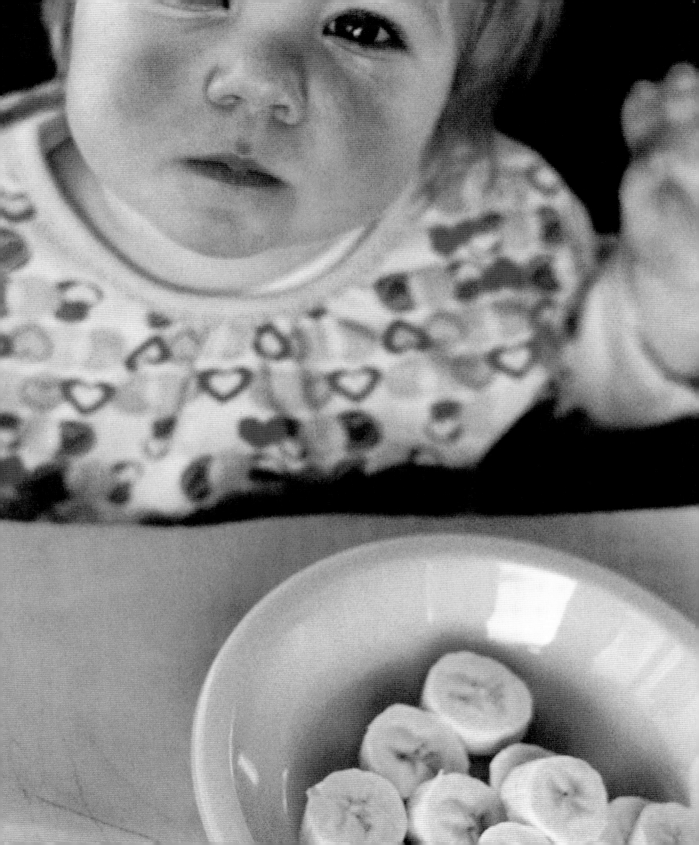

cooking with toddlers

As soon as babies take an interest in their surroundings, they notice more than you think. Those fed from a jar may well think that's where all food comes from. But if your baby or toddler sees you peeling a banana or scraping and cooking a carrot and then mashing it on a plate before you offer it to her on a spoon, she'll quickly understand that there is more to mealtimes than opening a packet.

What's more, home-cooking means that she will see and smell the food before she eats it, which helps to build up her appetite. It causes her body to start producing saliva and other digestive juices that will all help in the swallowing and digestion of the food.

HOW TO GET THEM INVOLVED

If your toddler can put some grapes in a little bowl, wash a new potato, or pretend to cut a carrot (with a plastic knife), she'll engage with the food and enjoy the story behind it. Even if you're just peeling an apple for her, let her see you doing it and involve her as much as you can. In my experience, if a toddler sees there's a story behind food, she's more likely to want to eat it. From a very early age my daughter Maya took a keen interest in what was going on at the sink and on the cooker. Ever since she's been old enough, she's had her own little table where she can mess around with food.

GROW FOOD TOGETHER

I'm planning our new garden at the moment and intend to give my daughter her own spot there, so she can start growing a few carrots or lettuce leaves – things that are really easy to grow. But you don't need an outdoor space: get your child to grow some mustard and cress on a wet wodge of tissues on the windowsill, or beansprouts in a jar. Everything you can do to get your child in touch with where food comes from will help her build up a healthy respect for the food she eats. If children can see that food takes time, they'll have more patience in the long run.

'If your toddler can put some grapes in a bowl or wash a new potato, she'll engage with the food and enjoy the story behind it.'

savoury recipes

carrot, swede and savoy cabbage purée

7+
MONTHS

For adults, this is great with roast meats, and delicious reheated the next day in a frying pan and topped with a fried egg.

makes 6 baby portions

1 large carrot, roughly chopped

1 swede, roughly chopped

1 teaspoon fresh rosemary leaves

½ a Savoy or dark green cabbage, thinly sliced

olive oil (optional)

freshly ground black pepper (optional)

1 Put the carrot and swede into a saucepan with the rosemary leaves and cover with water. Bring to the boil and cook for about 10 minutes, until you can almost push a knife through the swede. Add the cabbage and cook for another 5 minutes.

2 Drain the vegetables and whiz in a food processor to a coarse or smooth texture, depending on the age of your baby. For babies over 7 months, add a dash of olive oil and season with freshly ground black pepper if you wish.

OTHER GOOD ROOT VEG PUREES

Simply cook and purée together any of the following combinations for babies from 6 months:

parsnip and potato
parsnip and apple
parsnip, swede and turnip
parsnip, carrot and potato
swede and carrot
beetroot and carrot

celeriac and red cabbage purée

This pinky purple purée goes well with good-quality sausages, home-made beefburgers or an oily fish such as salmon for the rest of the family.

7+
MONTHS

makes 6 baby portions

1 medium celeriac, peeled and cut into small chunks

1 bay leaf

2 garlic cloves, sliced

a few sprigs of fresh thyme

¼ of a red cabbage, thinly sliced

olive oil, vegetable oil or unsalted butter

freshly ground black pepper

1 Cook the celeriac in boiling water with the bay leaf, garlic and thyme for about 10 minutes, until you can almost push a knife through the celeriac. Add the cabbage and boil for a further 9 minutes.

2 Drain and discard the herbs. Purée with a little olive, other vegetable oil or unsalted butter, and season with freshly ground black pepper.

OTHER GOOD WINTER VEG PUREES

Cook and purée any of the following combinations for babies from 6 months:

brussels sprouts with frozen peas

red cabbage with apple

sweet potato, carrot and ginger purée with sesame seeds

If your family has a history of allergies, omit the sesame seeds and replace the sesame oil with olive oil.

9+
MONTHS

2 sweet potatoes, peeled and sliced

2 medium carrots, sliced

a thumb-sized piece of fresh ginger, peeled and thinly sliced

1 teaspoon toasted sesame seeds

2 teaspoons toasted sesame oil

1 Put the sweet potatoes, carrots and ginger into a pan of cold water and bring to the boil. Reduce the heat and simmer, with the lid on, until the vegetables are tender and you can push a knife through them (10–15 minutes).

2 Drain well and tip into a food processor. Add the seeds and oil and blitz until either smooth or a little textured, depending on the age of your baby.

OTHER GOOD SWEET POTATO PUREES

For babies from 6 months, simply cook and purée the following with no other ingredients :

sweet potato and parsnip

sweet potato and carrot

breakfast

porridge

7+
MONTHS

Porridge is one of the healthiest breakfasts around. Buy the cereals you like for all the family and simply whiz them in a food processor to a suitable texture for your baby. Whiz enough for a few days at a time, and store in an airtight container.

1 cup of grain (choose from rolled oats, millet, quinoa, rice flakes)

1 cup of milk (you can use rice, soya, follow-on, oat milk)

¾ cup of water

the cup measurement is not specific as long as you use the same cup for each ingredient.

1 Put everything into a saucepan, pop it on to a gentle heat and stir for about 5 minutes, until you have a thick creamy porridge.

2 Dish up and add the topping of your baby's choice. If you prefer to keep it simple, add apple concentrate to sweeten and yoghurt to make it rich and creamy.

GOOD THINGS TO ADD TO PORRIDGE

Sweeten your baby's porridge with **fresh fruits** or **puréed dried fruits** for babies over 9 months. **Honey** can be added for babies over 12 months.

apricot and fig fruit compote

9+
MONTHS

Use any dried fruits you think your family will enjoy.

makes 6 baby portions

400g/14oz dried apricots and figs (you could use other fruits such as prunes and sultanas if you wish)

1 Pop the fruit into a saucepan with a lid and add just enough boiling water to cover. Let the fruits sit until they start to swell up and plump out, then simmer for 20 minutes, or until the fruits are completely softened. Leave to cool and purée in a liquidizer.

2 The compote will keep in an airtight jar in the fridge for up to a week – perfect for adding to cereals, spooning into yoghurt or filling pancakes.

fruity family muesli

Although there are some really good mueslis and other cereals in the supermarkets and health-food stores, others are pretty high in salt and sugar. I don't think anything beats making your own – you can use whichever cereals and dried fruits your toddler likes, and you can change the blend as he grows older and can manage larger pieces. Avoid nuts and seeds if there is any family history of allergies.

makes 650g/1lb 7oz

200g/7oz rolled oats

100g/3½oz millet flakes

25g/1oz rye flakes

100ml/3½fl oz apple juice

25g/1oz sesame seeds (not suitable for those with a family history of allergy, see page 208)

25g/1oz linseeds (see above)

75g/2½oz unsulphured dried apricots, finely chopped

75g/2½oz figs, tough stalks removed, finely chopped

50g/2oz stoned dates, chopped

25g/1oz raisins

25g/1oz sultanas

1 Preheat the oven to 180°C/350°F/gas mark 4.

2 Put the oats, millet flakes, rye flakes, apple juice, sesame seeds and linseeds into a bowl and mix thoroughly. Tip into a roasting tray and spread out evenly. Bake on the middle shelf of the oven for 25–30 minutes, until the mixture starts to turn golden brown. Stir the flakes a couple of times during cooking to ensure that they brown evenly. Take the tray out of the oven and allow to cool, and stir in the dried fruits. You can store the muesli in an airtight container for up to a month.

FOR BABIES 7-12 MONTHS OLD

Place the oats, millet flakes and rye flakes into a food processor and blitz to the consistency your baby can manage. Serve with milk. For 9 months plus you can then add the dried fruits, all finely chopped, and the seeds, or alternatively grated apple, and serve with fruit compote or just some milk.

home-made ricotta

This recipe is from my dear friend Patricia Michelson, who owns the fantastic cheese shop in London, La Fromagerie, and is one of the most inspiring foody mums I know. The cheese must be made in one session from start to finish – for this amount of milk count on it taking 1½ hours, although much of this time is semi-unattended cooking; you should be in or near the kitchen, but you don't need to hover over the stove. The recipe may seem daunting, but it is really quite easy. Because cheesemaking is unfamiliar to many, the instructions lead you through the process step by step. Once you are used to it, it really is a doddle. Heating the milk slowly gives a soft ricotta curd time to develop. Fast heating hardens the curd, producing a very different cheese.

**makes approximately
425g/15oz**

3 litres/5 pints organic whole milk (cow's or goat's)

175ml/6fl oz organic full-cream live yoghurt (cow's or goat's); use organic double cream instead if you want a richer cheese

75ml/3fl oz fresh lemon juice

1 Put all the ingredients into a heavy saucepan with a non-reactive interior and stir. Set the pan on a heat-diffusing pad over a medium-low heat and cook for 40 minutes, or until the milk reaches 170°F/77°C on an instant-reading thermometer (the glass one for floating on liquids is best and can be bought from shops selling home winemaking/beer equipment, specialist food equipment stores or hardware shops). Keep the heat low. To keep the curd large, do not stir more than three or four times. If you lift it with the spatula, you will see sand-like particles of milk forming as the clear whey begins to separate from the curd.

2 As the milk comes close to 170°F/77°C, the curds will be larger, about the size of an uncooked lentil. When the temperature reaches 170°F/77°C, turn the heat up to medium. Do not stir. Take 6–8 minutes to bring the mixture to 205°F/96°C at the centre of the pot. The liquid whey will be almost clear. By the time the cheese comes to 205°F/96°C the curd should mound on the spatula like a soft white custard. It will be on the verge of boiling, with the surface looking like mounds about to erupt. Turn off the heat and let it stand for 10 minutes.

3 Line a colander with a double thickness of dampened muslin cheesecloth (untreated cheesecloth can be bought at hardware shops selling jam-making equipment). Turn the mixture into it and let it drain for 15 minutes or until the drained cheese is thick. Place the cheese in a covered storage container and refrigerate until needed. You can use the whey to add to scone or muffin ingredients.

GOOD THINGS TO ADD TO RICOTTA

soft fruits (puréed for younger babies)

muesli (ground until your baby is ready for it to be chopped)

puréed apple

puréed apricots

for lunch – mix it with garlic and chives to make a savoury soft cheese. Ricotta is exactly how the milk forms in the tummy as it is digested, and so, added to other puréed solids such as carrot or a little potato, it forms the start of your baby's journey to the next stage of development.

pumpkin and sweetcorn soup

The natural sweetness of squash makes this soup a favourite with babies and toddlers. If you're short on time, skip roasting the pumpkin.

7+
MONTHS

makes 8 baby or 2 adult and 4 baby portions

750g/1½lb pumpkin or butternut squash (prepared weight), peeled, seeds removed, flesh chopped into 2cm/¾ inch dice

a dash of olive oil

25g/1oz butter

1 medium onion, chopped

2 sticks of celery, chopped

1 medium-sized leek, washed and chopped

2 garlic cloves, finely chopped

500g/1lb 2oz cooked sweetcorn, tinned (rinsed and drained) or frozen

freshly ground black pepper

250ml/9fl oz semi-skimmed or full cream milk (you could use soya or any type of oat/rice milk)

700ml/1¼ pints low-salt vegetable or chicken stock (use water for babies under 12 months)

wholemeal croutons and a swirl of natural yoghurt, to serve (optional)

1 Preheat the oven to 180°C/350°F/gas mark 4. Put the diced pumpkin or squash on a baking tray, drizzle with a little olive oil and roast for about 30–40 minutes, until the pumpkin is golden brown.

2 Meanwhile, melt the butter in a saucepan. Add the onion, celery and leek and soften them for about 6 minutes. Add the garlic and continue to cook for a further 2 minutes. Add the roasted pumpkin (or butternut squash) and the cooked sweetcorn, give everything a good stir, and season with freshly ground black pepper.

3 Put the lid on the pan and let the vegetables cook over a low heat for about 10 minutes, then pour in the milk and stock or water and simmer gently for about 20 minutes more. Put the lid on while it simmers and watch carefully, as it can easily boil over – turn it down low, or perhaps leave a little gap between the lid and the pan.

4 When the soup is ready, whiz it in a blender or purée it using a stick blender, leaving a little bit of texture (it doesn't need to be absolutely smooth). Serve with some wholemeal bread croutons if your baby is ready for chewing and, if you like, a swirl of thick natural yoghurt.

carrot and orange soup

The orange gives this soup a healthy dose of vitamin C – and babies love dishes that combine fruit and veg.

7+
MONTHS

makes 6 baby or 2 adult and 2 baby portions

a good-sized dash of olive oil

1 large onion, finely chopped

1 garlic clove, finely chopped

1 medium potato, peeled and finely chopped

2 sticks of green celery, finely chopped

750g/1½lb carrots, finely chopped

1 large unwaxed orange, washed

1.5 litres/2¾ pints low-salt chicken or vegetable stock (use water for babies under 12 months)

freshly ground black pepper

1 Heat the olive oil gently in a large pan and add the onion and garlic. Fry for a couple of minutes until golden, then add the potato, celery and carrots. Turn down the heat, cover the pan and cook for 5 minutes.

2 Meanwhile, grate the zest from the orange and squeeze the juice. Set aside 2 tablespoons of juice and add the rest to the vegetables with the stock or water. Bring to the boil, cover the pan and simmer for 20 minutes, until the vegetables are tender. Once cooked, remove from the heat, liquidize, add the reserved orange juice and season to taste with plenty of freshly ground black pepper.

beetroot and carrot soup

Babies and toddlers will love the bright colour of this soup.

7+
MONTHS

makes 4 baby or 1 adult and 2 baby portions

olive oil

1 onion, chopped

2 carrots, chopped

1 garlic clove, finely chopped

2 sticks of celery, chopped

2 raw beetroots, peeled and roughly chopped

1 medium parsnip, chopped

1 large potato or sweet potato, peeled and diced

1 litre/1¾ pints low-salt vegetable stock (use water for babies under 12 months)

2 bay leaves

1 Heat a little olive oil in a medium-sized pan and add the onion, carrots, garlic and celery. Fry gently for about 5 minutes, until the vegetables start to turn soft, but not too golden. Add the beetroots, parsnip, potato or sweet potato, stock or water and bay leaves. Bring to the boil, half cover the pan and simmer for about 30 minutes.

2 Remove from the heat and leave to cool for 5 minutes. Remove the bay leaves, then, using a hand-held blender, whiz up until smooth and creamy.

dips

hummus

Although there's some pretty OK hummus out there in the supermarkets I don't think ready-made hummus compares with home-made – you get a much thicker, nuttier-tasting dip when you make your own. You can use tinned chickpeas, in which case you need a 400g/14oz tin, but the taste is much better with soaked and freshly cooked ones.

9+
MONTHS

makes 6 baby or 6 adult and 2 baby portions

125g/4½oz dried chickpeas

a squeeze of lemon juice

2 tablespoons tahini (not suitable for children with a family history of allergies, see page 208)

2 garlic cloves, finely chopped

3 tablespoons olive oil

freshly ground black pepper

2 tablespoons of finely chopped parsley or sesame seeds (optional, and see above)

1 Put the chickpeas in a saucepan, cover them with boiling water and put to one side to soak for 2–3 hours. Drain the chickpeas and rinse well, then return them to the pan and cover with plenty of fresh water. Bring them to the boil, half cover the pan and simmer gently for about 1½–2 hours, until tender. Drain, reserving 150ml/5fl oz of the cooking liquid.

2 Pop the chickpeas into a blender with the lemon juice, tahini, garlic, olive oil and half the cooking liquid. Whiz until smooth or keep it a little crunchier, depending on how your baby likes it, adding a little of the reserved cooking liquid if the hummus is too thick. Season to taste with freshly ground black pepper and, if you need more sharpness, a little extra lemon juice. You can also add fresh herbs to the hummus, such as a couple of tablespoons of finely chopped fresh parsley or coriander, or even top it with some toasted seeds if you wish.

babaganoush

9+
MONTHS

Toddlers love to dip chunks of raw vegetables such as carrots into babaganoush. It's also good for spreading on toast, as a topping for jacket potatoes or rice cakes, or served in pitta breads with sliced tomatoes and cucumber.

makes 3 baby or 1 adult and 1 baby portion

1 large aubergine

2 heaped teaspoons tahini (not suitable children with a family history of allergies, see page 208)

150ml/5fl oz thick, plain Greek-style yoghurt

2–3 tablespoons lemon juice

freshly ground black pepper

1 Preheat the oven to 200°C/400°F/gas mark 6. Pierce the aubergine with a fork several times. Pop it on a baking tray and put it into the oven to roast for about 45 minutes. Remove from the oven and slice lengthways, keeping the stalk intact.

2 Put the aubergine pieces into a colander and leave to cool – the excess liquid will drain off, which prevents the dip from being too mushy. When cold, peel off the skin and discard. Remove the stalk end and pop the aubergine flesh into a liquidizer with the tahini, yoghurt and lemon juice. Whiz and season with black pepper.

egg 'majonaise'

7+
MONTHS

Since raw egg is off the menu, why not try this adaptation? This eggy topping is easy, soft and delicious to eat, and great for topping soft rolls for toddler's birthday parties – as I found out on my daughter Maya's fourth birthday. The children wolfed it down!

makes 3 baby or 1 adult and 1 baby portion

2 hard-boiled free-range eggs

4 tablespoons Greek-style thick yoghurt, fromage frais or ricotta

½ teaspoon creamed horseradish (you can buy in jars from supermarkets)

freshly ground black pepper

1 Put the eggs into a bowl and crush into small pieces with a fork, add the remaining ingredients and mix together. Mash up for younger babies if necessary.

broad bean and dill salad

Salad isn't usually a favourite food for toddlers, but they love this one.

12+ MONTHS

makes 6 toddler or 2 adult and 2 toddler portions

375g/12oz shelled broad beans

250g/9oz tiny baby carrots

8 spring onions, trimmed

250g/9oz shelled garden peas

50g/2oz bag of ready-prepared rocket

10cm/4-inch piece of cucumber, sliced thinly

1 ripe avocado, stoned, peeled and sliced

a handful of alfalfa sprouts (optional)

handful of fresh dill, roughly chopped

plenty of freshly ground black pepper

DRESSING

3 tablespoons lemon juice

grated zest of 1 unwaxed lemon

8 tablespoons olive oil

1 teaspoon Dijon mustard

1 To skin the broad beans, put them into a bowl and pour boiling water over them. When cool enough to handle, simply slip off the outer skin to reveal the beautiful vivid green inner bean in two halves. As you skin them, place them in a large salad bowl.

2 Put the carrots in a steamer over a pan of simmering water. Steam them for 4 minutes, then add the spring onions and peas and steam for a further 3–4 minutes.

3 Meanwhile, place all the dressing ingredients in a screw-top jar, put on the lid and shake vigorously.

4 When the vegetables are tender but still retaining their bite, remove them from the steamer and add them to the salad bowl. Drizzle over the dressing and mix well. Allow the veggies to cool slightly, then add the rocket, cucumber, avocado, alfalfa and dill. Season to taste with black pepper and serve straight away.

carrot and cumin salad with coriander

10+
MONTHS

This is a delicious and easy-to-make salad that children enjoy. You could add some grated cucumber, for a change – in which case, use half and half carrots and cucumber.

makes 6 toddler or 2 adult and 2 toddler portions

⅔ teaspoon cumin seeds (not suitable for children with a family history of allergies, see page 208)

1 garlic clove, coarsely chopped

3 tablespoons lemon juice

½ teaspoon caster sugar

1 tablespoon olive oil

500g/1lb 2oz really fresh firm carrots

1 small bunch of fresh coriander, freshly chopped

freshly ground black pepper

1 Toast the cumin seeds in a dry non-stick pan – it takes just a couple of minutes to warm them up and bring out their great flavour. Grind them in a pestle and mortar, then add the garlic and pound again until you have a paste. Mix the lemon juice, sugar and olive oil into the garlic mixture.

2 Grate the carrots finely (for speed you can use the grater blade of a food processor) and toss them in the cumin dressing with the coriander and a sprinkling of black pepper.

roasted butternut squash, feta and rocket salad

The sweet-savoury flavour of this salad is loved by toddlers.

12+ MONTHS

makes 3 toddler or 1 adult and 2 toddler portions

½ a medium-sized butternut squash, cut into chunks

olive oil

a small bag of ready-washed rocket

125g/4½oz feta cheese

1 ripe avocado, sliced

¼ of a cucumber, sliced

1 spring onion, thinly sliced

lemon juice

freshly ground black pepper

hummus (optional; not suitable for children with a family history of allergies, see page 208)

1 Preheat the oven to 200°C/400°F/gas mark 6. Put the pieces of butternut squash on a baking tray, drizzle with a little olive oil and cook in the oven for about 30 minutes, until golden brown and soft. Remove the seeds and set aside to cool.

2 Meanwhile, put the rocket into a salad bowl and crumble in the feta. Add the avocado, cucumber and spring onion. Remove the flesh from the squash, cut into bite-sized chunks, then add it to the salad – don't worry if it breaks up, as this will make the salad deliciously creamy. Drizzle with a little oil and freshly squeezed lemon juice, and scatter over plenty of black pepper.

3 You may like to serve the salad with a dollop of hummus on the side. Any leftovers can be popped into the fridge for the next day.

quick and easy warming chicken and tomato couscous

10+ MONTHS

Although you may think that toddlers won't like anything spicy, that isn't necessarily the case. Maya loves food with a bit of a kick – and this kick is gentle. If you're making it for adults only, you could use a stronger curry paste.

makes 5 toddler or 2 adult and 1 toddler portions

2 skinless chicken breasts
olive oil
150g/5½oz couscous
200ml/7fl oz boiling water
1 tablespoon mild curry paste
juice of 1 lime
2 handfuls of cherry tomatoes, quartered

YOGHURT DRESSING
a small pot of natural yoghurt
¼ a cucumber, finely chopped
1 heaped tablespoon freshly chopped mint

1 First get your grill or grill-pan very hot. Drizzle the chicken breasts with a little olive oil and grill or chargrill for 10–15 minutes, turning once, until cooked through.

2 While the chicken is cooking, pop the couscous into a large bowl. Measure out the boiling water and stir in the curry paste and lime juice. Pour the liquid over the couscous and cover it with clingfilm. After 5 minutes, fluff up the couscous with a fork and add the cherry tomatoes. In a separate small bowl mix the dressing ingredients.

3 Remove the chicken breasts from the grill and cut into small pieces if you have a toddler joining you. Serve with warm couscous and a spoonful of the yoghurt dressing.

crunchy chicken fingers

Get your toddler to help with this recipe if you've got the time.

makes 5 toddler or 2 adult
and 1 toddler portions

400g/14oz skinless chicken
breasts

40g/1½oz porridge oats

40g/1½oz wholemeal
breadcrumbs

finely grated zest of ¼ of an
unwaxed lemon

1 tablespoon freshly chopped
fresh parsley or tarragon

freshly ground black pepper

1 medium egg

olive or other vegetable oil

1 Preheat the oven to 170°C/325°F/Gas mark 3. Cut the chicken into strips about 8cm x 2 cm/3 inches x ¾-inch. Mix the oats and breadcrumbs in a large mixing bowl. Add the lemon zest and chopped herbs and season with black pepper. In a separate bowl beat the egg.

2 Dip the chicken strips first into the egg, then into the dry ingredients, making sure they're coated completely. Heat a good dash of oil in a large frying pan and fry the chicken on one side until the coating turns golden brown – at which point, turn it over and brown the other side. You may need to cook the chicken strips in batches, adding a little more oil to the pan for the second batch.

3 Transfer the chicken strips to a greased baking tray and put into the oven to cook thoroughly, which usually takes about 15–20 minutes. Cut into small pieces for babies and young toddlers.

family chicken with bay leaves

A great recipe for the whole family.

12+
MONTHS

makes 5 toddler or 2 adult and 1 toddler portions

1 x 1.5kg/3lb 5oz chicken, cut into 8 pieces

2 tablespoons extra virgin olive oil

1 mediuœm onion, finely chopped

2 stalks of celery, washed and finely chopped

1 large garlic clove, finely chopped

2 tablespoons finely chopped flat-leaf parsley

4 bay leaves

Freshly ground black pepper

200ml/7fl oz white wine or low-salt chicken stock (use water for babies under 12 months)

1 Rinse the chicken pieces in cold water and pat thoroughly dry with kitchen paper. Heat the olive oil in a large non-stick sauté pan. When the oil is hot, add the chicken pieces and brown really well on both sides. Remove from the pan and set aside.

2 Add the onion and celery to the pan and cook until slightly golden. Add the garlic, parsley and bay leaves and continue to cook for a further minute, then return the chicken pieces to the pan and season well with freshly ground black pepper.

3 Add the white wine or stock and bring to the boil. Bubble for 1 minute to allow the alcohol to evaporate, then cover the pan and cook over a very low heat for about 35–45 minutes, until the meat comes easily away from the bone and is cooked through. Turn the chicken pieces from time to time, and if they start to stick, add 2 to 3 tablespoons of water.

4 Take the chicken off the bone and either mince or cut into small pieces before serving it to babies and toddlers.

home-made burgers

You can make these burgers with minced lamb or pork instead of beef, or even with a mixture of different meats. They freeze well uncooked.

makes 12 burgers, each weighing 75–100g/3–4oz

1 tablespoon olive oil, plus a little for frying the burgers

1 red onion, finely chopped

750g/1½lb minced beef (ideally extra lean, 5% fat, and not more than 10%)

2 teaspoons English mustard

a pinch of cumin seeds, ground

½ tablespoon coriander seeds, ground

1 large egg, beaten

75g/2½oz wholemeal breadcrumbs

75g/2½oz freshly cooked wild rice

plenty of freshly ground black pepper

a squeeze of lemon juice

1 Heat the olive oil in a frying pan and add the onion. Cook gently until it softens, but don't let it colour. Remove from the pan and cool. Mix all the other ingredients together in a bowl, then add the onion and mix well. It's easiest to use your hands. Shape the mixture into patties and chill in the fridge for 20 minutes or so. You can freeze the burgers at this point.

2 Heat a small glug of olive oil in a non-stick frying pan and fry the burgers gently for 8-10 minutes on each side, or until cooked through.

3 For older toddlers I serve the burgers in fresh crusty wholemeal buns or in an Italian bread such as focaccia, with some sliced ripe tomato, very thinly sliced red onion, fresh salad leaves (I like bitter leaves such as rocket) and sliced ripe avocado, but you can of course mash them or slice them up easily for toddlers and serve them with mashed vegetables or pasta – they're incredibly versatile.

slow-cook beef casserole

A deliciously rich stew for adults and toddlers alike.

12+
MONTHS

**makes 5 toddler or 2 adult
and 1 toddler portions**

800g/1lb 12oz lean beef steak,
cut into large chunks

freshly ground black pepper

2 tablespoons olive oil

50g/2oz smoked bacon, diced

12 shallots, peeled but left
whole

2 sticks celery, roughly
chopped

2 medium carrots, thickly
sliced

4 garlic cloves, chopped

750ml red wine (preferably
Burgundy for adults!), or
low-salt beef stock

1 tablespoon tomato purée

1 bouquet garni (sprigs of
thyme, rosemary and
flat-leafed parsley)

12 small dark mushrooms,
halved if large

2 medium courgettes, sliced
thickly

1 Preheat the oven to 150°C/300°F/gas mark 2. Season the beef with freshly ground black pepper. Heat half the olive oil in a large frying pan over a high heat. Fry the beef in two batches until well browned and transfer to a casserole dish.

2 Heat the remaining olive oil in the frying pan, add the bacon, shallots, celery and carrots and fry until golden brown. Add the garlic and continue to cook for a further minute. Tip into the casserole dish. Place the frying pan back over the heat and pour in half the red wine. Bring to the boil and stir well with a wooden spoon to incorporate any caramelized bits on the bottom of the pan. Pour into the casserole and add the remaining wine, tomato purée and bouquet garni. Bring to the boil, cover with a tight-fitting lid and cook in the oven for 1½ hours.

3 Sauté the mushrooms in a little olive oil and add to the casserole with the sliced courgettes. Put back into the oven for a further 1¼ hours, or until the meat is tender. Mash for younger babies or chop for older babies and toddlers.

bolognaise sauce

This is my favourite bolognaise sauce; deep-tasting and rich, it's perfect comfort food.

makes 5 toddler or 2 adult and 1 toddler portions

3 tablespoons good olive oil

50g/2oz smoked streaky bacon, diced

1 onion, finely diced

2 sticks of celery, finely diced

2 carrots, finely diced

2 garlic cloves, finely chopped

1 teaspoon fresh thyme leaves

1 bay leaf

1 teaspoon dried oregano

1 x 400g/14oz tin of chopped tomatoes

1 tablespoon tomato purée

1½ teaspoons anchovy essence or anchovy sauce (optional – for babies 12 months plus)

1 tablespoon Worcestershire sauce (optional – for babies 12 months plus)

875/1¾lb good-quality lean minced beef (ideally 5% fat, maximum 10%)

125g/4½oz fresh chicken livers, finely chopped (optional)

375ml/13fl oz water

375ml/13fl oz dry red wine

1 litre/1¾ pints chicken, beef or lamb stock

freshly ground black pepper

1 Heat 1 tablespoon of olive oil in a large, heavy-based pan and fry the bacon until it's crisp and has released some natural fat. Add the onion, celery, carrots, garlic, thyme, bay leaf and oregano and cook over a medium heat until the vegetables have softened. Add the tinned tomatoes and tomato purée and the anchovy essence and Worcestershire sauce if using, and stir.

2 In a separate large frying pan, heat another tablespoon of olive oil and fry the meat in small batches until browned, breaking up any lumps with the back of a wooden spoon. Drain off any fat and add the browned meat to the tomato mixture.

3 Add the remaining oil to the same frying pan and fry the chicken livers until brown and crusty. Add them to the meat mixture. Deglaze the frying pan with some of the red wine, scraping any bits from the bottom. Pour this wine, the remaining wine and the stock or water into the meat mixture. Bring to the boil, reduce the heat and simmer, stirring from time to time, for about 2 hours, topping up with water if the liquid reduces too much. Season with black pepper.

4 Leave to cool, then chill. When quite cold, lift off any solidified fat that forms on the top of the meat and discard. Serve with pasta, chopped into small pieces if necessary for your baby or toddler.

cod with roasted tomatoes

A highly nutritious dish for babies and toddlers.

**makes 4 baby or 1 adult
and 2 baby portions**

4 good-sized tomatoes on the
vine

1 tablespoon olive oil, plus a
little extra

a generous splash of balsamic
vinegar

freshly ground black pepper

175g/6oz skinless and
boneless cod fillet

lemon juice

a few sprigs of fresh thyme

1 Preheat the oven to 180°C/350°F/gas mark 4. Place the tomatoes in a small roasting tray and sprinkle with the olive oil, balsamic vinegar and some pepper.

2 Double check the fish for bones. Place it on a sheet of tin foil and brush it with a little olive oil. Squeeze over some lemon juice, sprinkle with black pepper and add the thyme sprigs. Fold in the sides of the foil and seal at the top to make a parcel. Place it in an ovenproof dish and bake for 15–20 minutes, until cooked.

3 Serve the fish with the tomatoes, mashed for younger babies or chopped up for older babies and toddlers.

fish fingers

10+
MONTHS

Toddlers seem to love all foods that come in mini-sized portions, and these crunchy fish fingers are perfect! They'll enjoy helping to make them, too.

makes 5 toddler or 2 adult and 1 toddler portions

400g/14oz skinless and boneless haddock or other white fish, such as coley or cod

50g/2oz porridge oats

50g/2oz wholemeal breadcrumbs

freshly ground black pepper

1 medium egg

olive or other vegetable oil

1 Preheat the oven to 170°C/325°F/gas mark 3. Cut the fish into strips about 8cm x 2cm/3 inches x ¾-inch. Double check for any bones. Mix the oats and breadcrumbs in a large bowl and season with black pepper. In a separate bowl beat the egg.

2 Dip the fish strips into the egg, then into the dry ingredients, making sure they're coated completely. Heat a good dash of oil in a large frying pan and fry the fish on one side until the coating turns golden brown – at which point, turn it over and cook the other side. You may need to do this in batches, adding more oil to the pan for the second batch.

3 Transfer the fish fingers to a baking tray and put into the oven to cook through, which usually takes about 10 minutes. Chop into small pieces if necessary.

fish pie with green veg

A real favourite with toddlers – and very nutritious.

8+
MONTHS

**makes 5 baby or 2 adult
and 1 baby portions**

2 medium-sized potatoes,
peeled and cut into 2cm/¾ inch
pieces

125g/4½oz peas, fresh or
frozen

olive oil

freshly ground black pepper

1 small onion, finely chopped

1 garlic clove, finely chopped

500g/1lb 2oz white skinless
and boneless fish fillets, skins
removed, chopped into small
pieces

2 handfuls of fresh spinach,
washed well and finely
chopped

1 handful of green beans,
trimmed and cut into 2.5cm/
1 inch lengths

4 tablespoons thick
Greek-style natural yoghurt

1 teaspoon Dijon mustard

1 Preheat the oven to 180°C/350°F/gas mark 4. Bring a pan of water to the boil, put in the potatoes and cook for 15 minutes, until very nearly cooked. Add the peas and cook for another couple of minutes, then remove from the heat and drain. Mash the potatoes and peas with a dash of olive oil and some freshly ground black pepper.

2 Double check the fish for any bones. Heat a dash of olive oil in a large frying pan, add the onion and garlic and cook until slightly golden. Add the fish and spinach and cook gently, stirring occasionally, but carefully. When cooked, take off the heat and double check the fish for any bones.

3 Blanch the green beans in boiling water and add to the fish mixture.

4 Return to the heat, add the yoghurt and mustard and gently heat through. Put the mixture into a greased ovenproof dish and top with the potato and pea mash. Pop into the oven until the pie is heated through and the top is crisp, crunchy and golden – about 15–20 minutes. Mash or chop, depending on the age of your baby.

smoked mackerel pâté

Smoked fish has some salt in it, but if everything else in your baby's diet is low-salt, a little bit of this every now and then is absolutely fine.

8+
MONTHS

makes 5 baby or 2 adult and 1 baby portions

200g/7oz smoked mackerel fillets (the non-peppery ones), with skins removed

200g/7oz ricotta (bought or home-made, see page 108)

a squeeze of fresh lemon juice

2 tablespoons natural yoghurt

freshly ground black pepper

1 Put all the ingredients into a food processor, season with freshly ground black pepper and whiz together until it is smooth.

sardine pâté

The sardine, like the mackerel in the pâté above, is a great omega-3-rich fish – perfect for babies and toddlers.

8+
MONTHS

makes 5 baby or 2 adult and 1 baby portions

1 x 200g/7oz tin of sardines in oil, drained well, bones and skin removed (a little fiddly, but it's worth it)

200g/7oz ricotta (bought or home-made, see page 108)

a large squeeze of fresh lemon juice

2 tablespoons natural yoghurt

freshly ground black pepper

1 Put all the ingredients into a food processor, season with freshly ground black pepper and whiz together until it is smooth.

bean and vegetable oat crumble

This is perfect toddler and family food. It can be fully prepared up to the baking stage in advance – just refrigerate and add 15 minutes to the baking time.

9+
MONTHS

makes 8 baby or 2 adult and 4 baby portions

olive oil

1 medium onion, thinly sliced

2 garlic cloves, finely chopped

1 x 400g/14oz tin of borlotti beans, drained and rinsed

1 x 400g/14oz tin of chickpeas, drained and rinsed

either 500ml/18fl oz of my roasted vegetable batch sauce (see page 149), or 2 x 400g/14oz tins of chopped tomatoes plus 4 tablespoons tomato purée

1 teaspoon Dijon mustard

1 teaspoon soy sauce (optional – not suitable for under 12 months

200g/7oz broccoli spears, cut into bite-sized florets

200g/7oz cauliflower, cut into bite-sized florets

2 small courgettes, thinly sliced

25g/1oz butter

freshly ground black pepper

150g/5½oz wholemeal breadcrumbs

a handful of porridge oats

a handful of seeds such as hemp, pumpkin, sunflower (not suitable for children with a family history of allergies, see page 208)

1 Preheat the oven to 180°C/350°F/ gas mark 4.

2 Heat a tablespoonful of olive oil in a large non-stick pan and add the onion and garlic. Cook for 5 minutes until softened, then add the beans, the chickpeas and the batch sauce or tinned tomatoes plus purée. Stir, then add the mustard and soy sauce. Cover and simmer for about 20 minutes.

3 Meanwhile, steam the broccoli, cauliflower and courgettes until *al dente*. Put them into a bowl and mash with the butter and black pepper.

4 Put the bean mix into a large ovenproof dish and spoon over the vegetable mash. Heat a little olive oil in a large non-stick frying pan and pop in the breadcrumbs, oats and seeds. Gently toast until they turn golden brown, stirring frequently to ensure even toasting. If using, sprinkle the toasted oat and seed mixture on top of the pie and bake in the oven for 20 minutes, until cooked right through and bubbling away. For younger babies (9 months plus) and toddlers omit the seeds from the topping and serve mashed up.

cauliflower cheese

8+
MONTHS

This is delicious on its own, but for older babies and toddlers you can add beans (green or the dried variety, soaked and cooked), peas, cherry tomatoes, mushrooms, or even some white fish, chopped hard-boiled egg, good-quality ham or cooked chicken.

makes 5 baby or 2 adult and 1 baby portions

1 cauliflower, trimmed and cut into 1cm/½ inch pieces

300g/10oz cream cheese or ricotta (see page 108)

1 teaspoon Dijon mustard

125g/4½oz Lancashire or other crumbly cheese

freshly ground black pepper

50g/2oz mature Cheddar cheese, grated

1 Cook the cauliflower in boiling salted water for about 8 minutes, or until tender. Drain, and return the cauliflower to the pan. Add the cream cheese and mustard and crumble in the Lancashire cheese. Season with a little salt and plenty of pepper. Pour into a shallow ovenproof dish or 6 ramekins and cover with the grated Cheddar.

2 Place under a preheated medium grill for 5 minutes, or until the top is golden-brown and the inside hot and bubbling. Chop or mash into small pieces if necessary.

herby courgettes

10+
MONTHS

It's good to introduce fresh zingy flavours to your children from an early age, and these courgettes are delicious – a change from plain vegetables. They go well with pasta, rice, any starch, or even with lentils.

makes 5 toddler or 2 adult and 1 toddler portions

500g/1lb 2oz courgettes

2 garlic cloves

2 tablespoons lemon juice

1 teaspoon Dijon mustard

freshly ground black pepper

4 tablespoons virgin olive oil

1 teaspoon each fresh chives, tarragon, parsley, rosemary leaves and dill

1 Trim the courgettes and, if they are small, slice them in half or quarters lengthways, depending on their size. Put them in the top of a steamer, pour in some boiling water and let them cook, covered, for about 10 minutes, until firm but tender.

2 Meanwhile, prepare the dressing. Crush the garlic with 1 teaspoon of the lemon juice in a pestle and mortar until it forms a creamy paste. Add the mustard, the remaining lemon juice and some black pepper. Pour in the oil and give everything a good stir, then add the herbs. Chop into small pieces if necessary.

stuffed courgettes

You can use this stuffing for many different vegetables – marrow, butternut squash or any other members of the squash family, cabbage leaves, mushrooms, or tomatoes. You just need to vary the final cooking time: a whole marrow for instance will take about 90 minutes, and the same for a whole squash, while tomatoes and cabbage leaves will take just 20–30 minutes.

makes 8 toddler or 2 adult and 4 toddler portions

500g/1lb 2oz courgettes

2 tablespoons olive oil

1 medium onion, finely chopped

2 stalks celery, finely chopped

2 large garlic cloves, crushed

6 large ripe tomatoes, finely chopped

1 small aubergine (about 200g/7oz), cut into bite-size pieces

2 tablespoons torn fresh basil

2 tablespoons fresh coriander, finely chopped

1 tablespoon tomato purée

8 anchovy fillets, well drained, finely chopped

1 tablespoon small capers

1 tablespoon wholemeal breadcrumbs

1 tablespoon porridge oats

½ tablespoon pumpkin or hemp seeds (optional)

juice of ½ a lemon

freshly ground black pepper

75g/2½oz mozzarella cheese, torn into pieces

25g/1oz Parmesan cheese, grated

1 Preheat the oven to 180°C/350°F/gas mark 4. Cut the courgettes in half lengthwise and with a sharp knife or teaspoon remove enough of the flesh to allow you to put some stuffing in. Chop the scooped-out flesh and put it with the courgette halves to one side.

2 Heat the olive oil in a large non-stick frying pan and gently fry the onion, celery and garlic until tender but not coloured. Add the tomatoes and simmer until soft – about 10 minutes. Add the aubergine and chopped courgette flesh and simmer for another 10 minutes, until squidgy. Add all the remaining ingredients except the cheeses, and season with pepper.

3 Arrange the courgettes snugly in an ovenproof dish. Fill each of the courgettes with the stuffing and top with the mozzarella and Parmesan. Don't worry if you have some stuffing left over; keep it in the fridge and use it the next day. Cover with foil and cook for about 30 minutes, or until the courgettes are soft. Remove the foil and place under a preheated grill for about 5 minutes to crisp up the topping. Serve warm, chopped into small pieces. They're also delicious cold.

bubble and squeak

A really nutritious yummy dish for babies and toddlers.

10+
MONTHS

**makes 5 toddler or 2 adult
and 1 toddler portions**

butter for greasing

200g/7oz potatoes, peeled

125g/4½oz carrots

125g/4½oz parsnip, peeled

150g/5½oz squash, peeled and
deseeded

75g/2½oz spring greens or
dark green cabbage, shredded

2 tablespoons olive oil

freshly ground black pepper

1 Preheat the oven to 220°C/425°F/gas mark 7. Grease a small roasting tin or ovenproof gratin dish measuring 25 x 35cm (10 x 14 inches).

2 Cut the potatoes, carrots, parsnips and squash into even-sized pieces and steam or boil until soft but not mushy. Drain and dry well. Steam or boil the cabbage.

3 Put the root vegetables in a large bowl and pound with a potato masher. Add the cabbage, the olive oil and a sprinkling of black pepper. Spread the mixture in your greased baking tray or gratin dish and bake on the top shelf of the oven for 20–30 minutes, until crispy on top. Chop into small pieces if necessary.

spinach, pea and ricotta fritters

These tasty fritters are a great way to get your toddler to eat his veg!

10+
MONTHS

**makes 5 toddler or 2 adult
and 1 toddler portions**

250g/9 oz baby leaf spinach,
washed well and drained

125g/4½oz fresh or frozen peas
(thawed)

2 large eggs, beaten

5 tablespoons plain flour,
sifted

2 tablespoons porridge oats

250g/9oz ricotta cheese

freshly ground black pepper

vegetable oil

1 Heat a large frying pan and add the spinach, tossing the leaves until they wilt. If using fresh peas, add them now and cook for another 2 minutes. Drain the spinach and peas well, squeezing to remove any excess water. If you're using frozen peas, add them now. Place the spinach and peas in a mixing bowl and add the eggs, then the flour and oats, and finally the ricotta. Mix well and season with plenty of black pepper.

2 Heat a little vegetable oil in a non-stick frying pan. Drop large spoonfuls of the mixture into the pan and cook for 2 minutes on each side, until set and beginning to turn golden brown. Remove from the pan and keep warm in the oven. Chop into small pieces if necessary.

vegetable burgers

Toddlers will love these burgers!

9+

MONTHS

**makes 5 toddler or 2 adult
and 1 toddler portions**

2 x 400g/14oz tins of
chickpeas, drained and rinsed

3 plump garlic cloves, crushed

2 teaspoons ground coriander

2 teaspoons ground cumin

1 medium onion, chopped

2 tablespoons plain wholemeal
flour

juice of ½ a lemon

1 tablespoon chopped fresh
parsley

freshly ground black pepper

groundnut oil for deep-frying

1 Blend the chickpeas in a food processor with the garlic, spices and onion until smooth. Scoop into a bowl and stir in the flour, lemon juice and chopped parsley. Season with some pepper.

2 Stir the mixture thoroughly. With floured hands, shape the chickpea mixture into patties and shallow-fry them for 2 minutes on each side, until crisp and cooked through. It's important that the oil is really hot, or else they will break up and just soak up the oil rather than crisping up.

3 Serve the burgers hot, chopped up if necessary. Older toddlers will enjoy them stuffed into warm pitta bread, or sliced on top of jacket potatoes, or in soft rolls with a squirt of good tomato ketchup, or even some natural yoghurt. I'd also pop in some lettuce, sliced tomato and cucumber, as this is a fun way to get toddlers to tuck into vegetables. Finely chop or mash if necessary.

quick cabbage

This is a great idea for a quick supper.

12+

MONTHS

**makes 4 toddler or 1 adult
and 2 toddler portions**

olive oil

1 garlic clove, crushed

1 onion, finely chopped

50g/2oz streaky bacon, finely
chopped

450g/1lb green cabbage (or a
mixture of cabbage and kale),
washed and shredded

freshly ground black pepper

1 Heat a dash of olive oil in a non-stick wok or large frying pan and add the garlic and onion. Fry for a couple of minutes, until tender but not coloured. Add the bacon and fry for a further 2–3 minutes until the bacon crisps up and the onion is light golden. Throw in the cabbage and fry for about 8–10 minutes, stirring now and then, until it's cooked but still crispy. Season to taste with freshly ground black pepper. Chop into small pieces if necessary.

parmesan risotto

Risotto may sound as if it takes a long time, but if you have the energy to stand for 20 minutes, you should find the monotonous action of stirring a hypnotic stressbuster – rice seems to encourage the body to produce soporific hormones to wind us down!

makes 8 toddler or 2 adult and 4 toddler portions

1.5 litres/2¾ pints low-salt chicken or vegetable stock (use water for babies under 12 months)

2 shallots, finely chopped

2 tablespoons olive oil

25g/1oz unsalted butter

400g/14oz Carnaroli or Arborio rice

25g/1oz Parmesan cheese, grated

freshly ground black pepper

1 In a saucepan, heat the stock or water until it is simmering slowly and steadily.

2 In a heavy-bottomed risotto pan, sauté the shallots in the oil and half the butter until soft, but not brown. Add the rice, stirring until the grains are well coated, and cook for a couple of minutes to warm them through.

3 Now add the hot stock or water, a ladleful at a time, allowing the rice to soak up all the liquid before adding more. Keep adding stock until the rice is cooked, but not mushy – it should retain some texture. You may not need to add all the stock.

4 When the rice is cooked, turn off the heat. You can divide it into small portions and freeze it at this point. If you are going to eat it straight away, stir in the rest of the butter, sprinkle with grated Parmesan and season to taste with freshly ground black pepper.

GOOD THINGS TO ADD TO RISOTTO FOR 9+ MONTHS

spring – green beans, asparagus

summer – courgettes, peas

autumn – mushroom, squash

winter – parsnips

In most cases, simply add the ingredient 5–10 minutes before the end of the cooking time. Squash and parsnips should be added earlier – at the same time as the rice – or roasted.

potato, pea and courgette frittata

Frittatas are a great way to get your toddler to eat all sorts of vegetables!

**makes 6 toddler or 2 adult
and 2 toddler portions**

2 large potatoes (total weight
400g/14oz), peeled and cut
into 1cm/½ inch pieces

400ml/14fl oz low-salt
vegetable stock (use water for
babies under 12 months)

a dash of olive oil

1 garlic clove, finely chopped

1 small white onion, chopped

2 medium courgettes, thinly
sliced

200g/7oz frozen peas

a large handful of fresh
spinach or rocket

6 medium eggs

4 tablespoons whole milk

1 Preheat the oven to 170°C/325°F/gas mark 3. Grease a
20cm/8-inch round non-stick cake tin and line with foil.

2 Put the potatoes and water into a pan and bring to the
boil. Cook for about 10 minutes, until soft, then drain and
roughly mash with a fork until they're just a little mushy.

3 Heat the olive oil in a large non-stick frying pan.
Add the garlic and onion and fry until soft and only just
starting to colour. Add the courgettes and fry for another
3 minutes, until they start to soften. Add the potato
mixture, peas and spinach and cook for another couple
of minutes, then remove from the heat.

4 In a bowl, whisk together the eggs and milk. Stir in
the vegetable mixture, mixing gently, and pour into the
cake tin. Bake for about 20 minutes, then remove from the
oven and carefully pat down the top of the frittata, as this
helps to make it nice and compact when you eventually
tuck in. Pop the tin back in the oven for another 10–15
minutes, until it turns slightly golden brown and is set.
Remove from the oven, allow to cool slightly and serve hot
or cold, cut into small pieces.

simple daal

This is a good dish for getting babies used to some spice.

7+ MONTHS

makes 6 baby or 2 adult and 2 baby portions

250g/9oz red or yellow lentils (I like Tarka daal, which is a small lentil)

175g/6oz onions, finely chopped

2 garlic cloves, finely chopped

2 tablespoons olive oil

½ teaspoon turmeric

½ teaspoon ground ginger

½ teaspoon mild chilli powder

1 teaspoon ground cumin

900ml/1¾ pints water

1 cinnamon stick

½ a lemon

1 Rinse the lentils well to remove any bits and dirt (they can be a little rough and ready), and drain. Meanwhile, in a non-stick pan, sauté the onion and garlic in a little olive oil for a few minutes until they turn slightly golden. Add the spices and stir well. Cook gently for about 2 minutes.

2 Add the water, lentils, and cinnamon stick. Bring to the boil, then cover the pan and simmer for about 25–30 minutes, until the lentils are soft but not mushy. Remove the cinnamon stick and squeeze in the lemon juice.

3 Serve on its own (puréed if needs be) for younger babies, or with rice, pasta or pitta breads, which toddlers will use to scoop up the lentils.

easy tomato and basil sauce

A firm favourite with all the family – I make up a big batch that can be either frozen in portions or kept in a sealed container in the fridge.

7+ MONTHS

makes 8 baby or 2 adult and 4 baby portions

50g/2oz fresh small-leaved basil

2 x 400g/14oz tins of Italian plum tomatoes

6 garlic cloves, finely chopped

4 tablespoons olive oil

freshly ground black pepper

1 Remove the leaves from the basil and discard the stalks. Chop the leaves roughly. Drain, deseed and roughly chop the tomatoes and place them in a large saucepan. Set aside 1 tablespoon of the chopped basil leaves and add the remainder to the pan with the garlic and olive oil.

2 Cook the ingredients over a medium heat for about 30 minutes, stirring often to prevent them sticking to the pan. Season with plenty of freshly ground black pepper, throw in the reserved basil and stir. Whiz with a stick blender for younger babies.

roasted vegetable batch sauce

This is great served with pasta or as a base for other dishes.

7+
MONTHS

makes 2.25 litres/3¾ pints

625g/1¼lb ripe tomatoes

1 small butternut squash, seeds removed, chopped into large pieces

1 red pepper, seeds removed, cut into large chunks

olive oil

500ml/18fl oz low-salt vegetable stock (or water for babies under 12 months)

2 garlic cloves, finely chopped

1 onion, finely chopped

3 sticks of celery, finely chopped

2 carrots, finely chopped

2 courgettes, finely chopped

2 x 400g/14oz tins of plum tomatoes

1 Preheat the oven to 220°C/425°F/gas mark 7. Put the tomatoes, squash and red pepper in a deep roasting tray. Splash over a good glug of olive oil and put into the preheated oven on the middle shelf. Roast for about 30 minutes, until the vegetables are soft. Allow to cool for about 10 minutes, then carefully remove the skin from the squash and peppers and discard.

2 Put the squash flesh, tomatoes, pepper and any pan juices into a blender or liquidizer, along with 250ml/9fl oz of the stock or water. Blitz until smooth, then pass the sauce through a sieve (much quicker than peeling the tomatoes at the beginning – a good trick of the trade).

3 In a large saucepan, heat another splash of olive oil, add the garlic, onion, celery and cook for about 5 minutes. Add the carrots and courgettes and cook until all the vegetables are soft. Add the tinned tomatoes and the remaining stock or water, bring to the boil, cover and simmer for about 15 minutes. Then, using a stick blender, whiz the sauce until it's completely smooth.

4 Combine the two sauces.

pasta with green pesto

This is a great sauce for pasta! You can use watercress instead of rocket if you like, which would add some calcium and iron.

9+
MONTHS

makes 6 toddler or 2 adult and 2 toddler portions

2 garlic cloves, crushed

50g/2oz pine nuts (not suitable for children with a family history of allergies, see page 208)

25g/1oz fresh basil, leaves chopped

25g/1oz fresh rocket (or watercress), roughly chopped

4 tablespoons Parmesan or Pecorino Sardo cheese, grated

150ml/5fl oz olive oil

3 tablespoons fromage frais or ricotta

400g/14oz fresh or dried pasta

1 First, put a large pan of water on to boil for the pasta.

2 Grind the garlic and pine nuts in a food processor, adding the basil leaves and rocket a little at a time, until you have a paste. Stir in the Parmesan or Pecorino Sardo and gradually add the olive oil, mixing well. Finally add the fromage frais or ricotta.

3 When the pasta's ready, drain it and stir in the pesto sauce. Serve at once, chopped up if necessary.

pasta with walnuts and mushrooms

This is a good way to give children over 12 months some omega-3 fatty acids, which are great for hearts, joints and moods. If you omit the walnuts, double up on the quantity of mushrooms.

10+ MONTHS

makes 6 toddler or 2 adult and 2 toddler portions

400g/14oz fresh or dried pasta

175g/6oz walnuts, crushed into very fine pieces (not suitable for children with a family history of allergies, see page 208)

2 garlic cloves, finely chopped

4 tablespoons finely chopped fresh parsley

a glug of olive oil

200g/7oz dark flat mushrooms, finely chopped

freshly ground black pepper

1 First put a large pan of water on to boil for the pasta.

2 Place the walnuts in a food processor with the garlic and parsley and mix into a paste. Heat a little olive oil in a non-stick pan and fry the mushrooms until soft.

3 When the pasta's ready, drain it and mix well with the mushrooms and the herby walnut paste. Season to taste with black pepper. Chop into small pieces if necessary.

sweet
recipes

eggy bread with summer fruits

You can choose any soft fruits for this dish – blueberries, blackberries, plums and nectarines work just as well. In winter try stewed apples and pears.

10+
MONTHS

**makes 5 baby or 2 adult
and 1 baby portion**

2 large eggs

4 tablespoons milk

½ teaspoon cinnamon

a handful of strawberries

1 peach, stoned

a handful of raspberries

a small knob of butter

1 tablespoon vegetable oil

4 slices of wholemeal bread, not too thick

1 small banana, sliced

2 tablespoons of natural organic yogurt

1 In a large, shallow dish whisk together the eggs, milk and cinnamon.

2 Halve the strawberries and slice the peach. Put them into a small saucepan with the raspberries and place over a very low heat without any extra water until the peach slices start to soften at the edges.

3 Melt the butter with the oil in a frying pan over a medium heat. Dip your bread into the egg mix, making sure each side has soaked up the mixture, and fry for a couple of minutes on each side until golden. You may need to do this in batches depending on the size of your pan.

4 Serve with the sliced banana, the cooked fruits and a dollop of yoghurt. Chop the fruits and bread up into smaller pieces, depending on your baby's ability to chew.

raspberry and banana soya shake

6+
MONTHS

Soya is a great way to boost calcium intake, especially if your toddler can't tolerate dairy products. There is no comparison between the flavour of a home-made fruit shake and the bought variety. Simply add whatever fruits you have available (although raspberries and bananas make such a perfect combination that they are worth buying specially) to some soya yoghurt – delicious.

makes 2 baby portions

75g/2 ½ oz fresh raspberries

1 banana, roughly chopped

75ml/2 ⅛ fl oz calcium-enriched soya yoghurt

75ml/2 ⅛ fl oz calcium-enriched soya milk

1 Place the raspberries and banana in a liquidizer or food processor and whiz until smooth.

2 Add the soya yoghurt and soya milk and whiz again, until the ingredients are thoroughly mixed.

3 Pour the mixture through a sieve and serve at once.

OTHER GOOD FRUITS FOR SHAKES INCLUDE

strawberries

blueberries

mango

berry smoothie

6+
MONTHS

makes 2 baby portions

2 handfuls of frozen berries

150ml/5 fl oz Greek style natural yoghurt

a dash of milk

1 Whiz the berries in a blender or liquidizer with the yoghurt and milk for a delicious frozen smoothie.

puddings

rice pudding

8+
MONTHS

This is great warm or cold, with honey drizzled on top (if your baby's over 12 months), or with mashed banana, puréed fruits or compote. It can be frozen in small portions or tipped into little pots and filled up with chopped fresh fruits (if your baby's over 9 months).

makes 6 baby or 2 adult and 2 baby portions

1 x 410g/13oz tin of evaporated milk
500ml/18fl oz whole milk
110g/3½oz pudding rice
¼ teaspoon grated nutmeg
25g/1oz butter

1 Preheat the oven to 150°C/300°F/Gas mark 2. Lightly butter an ovenproof dish about 23cm/9 inches square and 5cm/2 inches deep.

2 Mix the evaporated milk and whole milk together in a jug. Put the rice into the ovenproof dish, pour in the liquid and stir well. Grate the nutmeg all over the surface and dot the butter on top in little flecks.

3 Bake on the centre shelf of the oven for 30 minutes, then slide the shelf out and give everything a good stir. Repeat the stirring after a further 30 minutes. Pop the dish back in the oven to cook for 45–50 minutes, this time without stirring. Mash if necessary.

chocolate and strawberry pud

This bread and butter pudding is packed with all the things that toddlers love – custard, chocolate and strawberries. It is packed with nutrients from the eggs, milk and fruit and is ideal as a weekend treat.

makes 6 toddler or 2 adult and 2 toddler portions

200g/7oz fresh strawberries

6 slices of wholemeal bread, crusts cut off

softened butter

100g/3½oz 70% cocoa bean chocolate, chopped

3 large eggs

2 tablespoons of pure fruit strawberry jam

300ml/½ pint milk

1 teaspoon vanilla extract

sprinkling of cocoa powder

1 Halve and set aside 6 small strawberries and slice the remainder. Spread the bread with the softened butter and lay 3 slices, buttered side up, on the work surface. Divide the sliced strawberries and chopped chocolate between the slices and top with the other slices of bread. Press together and cut each sandwich into quarters.

2 Butter a 1.5 litre/2¾ pint ovenproof dish and pack the sandwiches into it. Whisk the eggs and strawberry jam together in a bowl until smooth. Little by little add the milk and vanilla extract. Pour over the sandwiches and decorate with the remaining halved strawberries. Sieve over the cocoa powder and leave to rest for about 30 minutes to allow the custard to soak through the bread. Preheat the oven to 200°C/400°F/gas mark 6.

3 Bake the pudding on the middle shelf of the oven for about 30 minutes, until golden brown. You may need to loosely cover it with a sheet of foil towards the end to prevent it browning too quickly. Delicious warm or cold. Finely chop if necessary.

fruit jelly

This is a great recipe to make with toddlers as they can create individual jellies. It is a delicious pudding to have in the fridge for spontaneous tea-time parties. Serve on its own, or with natural yoghurt, home-made custard or ice cream.

makes 6 toddler or 2 adult and 2 toddler portions

600g/1lb 5oz fresh or frozen fruit, such as orange segments, raspberries, strawberries, kiwi, blueberries. Use either a mixture, or just one.

225ml/8fl oz freshly squeezed apple or orange juice

200ml/7 fl oz water

2 tbsp/30ml pure fruit spread, such as apple and pear

2 x 11g/¼ oz sachets of powdered vegetarian gelatine

juice of a lemon

1 Remove the pips, tops and tails from the fruit, and cut into bite-size pieces.

2 Line a 900g (2lb) loaf tin, or small jelly moulds, with cling film.

3 Combine the apple or orange juice and water. Heat half in a small pan until it begins to simmer. Add the fruit spread and gelatine. Stirring all the time, heat gently until the gelatine dissolves. Remove from heat and stir in the remaining liquid, including the lemon juice. Cool.

4 Put the fruit in layers or all mixed up into the prepared containers. Pour the jelly on top and refrigerate.

5 Wipe the sides of the mould with a warm dishcloth to loosen the outside of the jelly. Tip on to a serving plate. Remove the clingfilm (throw it away, as children might swallow it).

NOTES ON INGREDIENTS

Do not use pineapple as the acids inside the pineapple prevent the jelly from setting

pavlova

A real treat for all the family.

10+

MONTHS

makes 2 adult and 2 toddler portions

3 large, fresh (and they have to be very fresh) egg whites

175g/6oz caster sugar

1 teaspoon cornflour

1 teaspoon white wine vinegar

150ml/5fl oz whipping cream

150ml/5fl oz thick Greek-style yoghurt

500g/1lb 2oz fresh berries or other fresh fruits

a little icing sugar

1 Preheat the oven to 150°C/300°F/gas mark 2 and prepare a lightly oiled baking tray lined with baking silicone parchment which peels off easily – not baking paper, which will stick to the meringue.

2 Put the egg whites into a large clean, dry bowl. Whisk until stiff peaks form and you can turn the bowl over without the egg whites sliding out – but don't over-whisk, or your meringue will collapse. Whisk in the sugar a little at a time until it is all incorporated. Add the cornflour and vinegar, and continue to whisk for a few minutes, until the meringue mixture is thick and glossy.

3 Using a metal spoon, lightly spoon the mixture on to the baking sheet in big dollops, joining them together in a circle. (It's meant to look like a ballerina's frilly tutu!). Put the meringue into the oven, then immediately turn the temperature down to 140°C/275°F/gas mark 1. After an hour, turn the oven off. Leave the meringue in the cooling oven until it is completely cold; it will have dried out at the edges, but will still be squidgy in the middle.

4 Lift off the paper and place the meringue on a serving plate. Whip the cream and mix it with the yoghurt, spoon it into the middle of the meringue and throw the soft fruits on top. Dust with a little icing sugar. Chop up to serve if necessary. Chop up meringue if necessary when serving.

rhubarb fool

This is only suitable for 1-years-plus and you must use British Lion eggs.

12+ MONTHS

makes 6 toddler or 2 adult and 2 toddler portions

375g/13oz rhubarb, washed, trimmed and cut into 2cm/¾ inch lengths

50g/2oz caster sugar

juice of 1 orange

1 large egg white, whisked until stiff (make sure you use a British Lion seal egg, as the egg is not cooked, see page 51)

75ml/2½fl oz cream, whipped

75ml/2½fl oz thick natural yoghurt

1 Place the rhubarb, sugar and orange juice in a medium pan. Cover with a lid and bring to the boil, then reduce the heat and simmer until the rhubarb is really tender. Remove the lid and continue to cook for a further couple of minutes, until the rhubarb forms a purée and some of the liquid has been boiled off. Remove from the heat and allow to cool completely.

2 Meanwhile, in a large bowl, fold the egg white into the whipped cream and yoghurt. Fold in the cooled rhubarb, reserving a little for decoration.

3 Spoon the fool into individual glasses (if you've collected any of those little glass yoghurt pots, they're fun for 3-year-olds), or just pop it into their usual bowl and top with the reserved rhubarb.

blackberry and apple crumble

10+ MONTHS

makes 6 toddler or 2 adult and 2 toddler portions

250g/8oz plain white or wholemeal flour, sifted

110g/3¾oz butter, room temperature, cut into pieces

75g/2½oz soft light brown sugar

250g/9oz blackberries, fresh or frozen

750g/1lb 10oz cooking apples, peeled, cored and sliced

1 tablespoon golden caster sugar

1 Preheat the oven to 180°C/350°F/gas mark 4.

2 Put the flour, butter and light brown sugar into a food processor and whiz to crumbs. If you don't have a processor, put the flour into a large mixing bowl, add the butter and rub it in lightly, using your fingertips. When it's all crumbly, add the sugar and combine well.

3 Arrange the blackberries and apples in a shallow ovenproof baking dish. Sprinkle over the caster sugar and cover with the crumble mixture. Bake on the middle shelf of the oven for 40 minutes, until the crumble is golden on top and the fruit is tender. Chop up if necessary before serving.

pancakes

Pancakes are great to make. You can get your toddler involved with a bit of mixing, and they love to see you toss them – or not, as the case may be! You can use a sweet filling, as here, but they're equally good with a savoury one – hummus, avocado and cucumber, leftover roast chicken, cream cheese, you name it.

makes 12 pancakes in an 18cm/7 inch frying pan

125g/4½oz plain wheat flour, or use half and half with buckwheat flour

2 large eggs

200ml/7fl oz milk mixed with 75ml/2½fl oz water

50g/2oz butter

1 Sift the flour into a large mixing bowl and make a well in the centre. Break in the eggs and begin to whisk them, incorporating flour as you go. Gradually add small amounts of milk and water, whisking, until all the flour is in and the batter has the consistency of thin cream. You may not need all the liquid. Set aside for 20 minutes.

2 Melt the butter in a frying pan and add 2 tablespoons of it to the batter. Whisk it in, then pour the rest of the butter into a bowl and use it when you need to grease the pan, smearing it with kitchen paper. If you use a non-stick pan you will hardly need to grease between pancakes.

3 Get the pan really hot, then turn the heat down to medium and start making your pancakes: 2 tablespoons of batter should be enough for each pancake if you're using an 18cm/7 inch pan. If you spoon the batter into a ladle first, you can pour it into the hot pan in one go.

4 As soon as the batter hits the pan, tip it around to get the base evenly coated. It should take only half a minute or so to cook; lift the edge with a palette knife to check if it's golden underneath, then flip it over with a pan slice – cooking the other side will take a few seconds. Slide it onto a plate. Chop it up if necessary

GOOD THINGS TO SERVE PANCAKES WITH:

a sprinkling of caster sugar and a squeeze of lemon juice

pure fruit spread

apple purée

mashed banana

frozen strawberry yoghurt

Ideal for a hot, sunny day!

8+
MONTHS

**makes 6 baby or 2 adult
and 2 baby portions**

125g/4½oz strawberries, hulled

1 tablespoon apple concentrate

400ml/14fl oz natural full-fat
yoghurt

3 tablespoons double cream

1 teaspoon vanilla extract

1 Put the strawberries and apple concentrate into a blender and whiz to a purée.

2 If you have an ice-cream maker, just mix the strawberry purée, yoghurt, cream and vanilla extract, pop into the machine and follow the instructions.

3 If you don't have an ice-cream maker, mix the yoghurt with the cream and vanilla extract. Place in the freezer and chill for 30 minutes. Take the yoghurt out of the freezer and stir well to break down the ice crystals. Mix in the fruit purée, either completely, or gently, in strawberry ripple style. Pop back into the freezer for another 2 hours, remove and stir gently. Freeze for a further 2 hours.

chocolate banana 'lollies'

12+
MONTHS

In my last book, *Yummy*, I gave a recipe for frozen bananas and I had lots of letters saying how much kids loved them. Here's an indulgent step upwards, delicious for all the family and lovely to make with toddlers.

makes 10

2 medium bananas

10 cocktail sticks, sharp ends
removed

125g/4oz 70% cocoa bean
chocolate, broken into small
pieces

1 Peel the bananas, remove the brown end, and cut them on the diagonal into long oval slices – each banana makes about 5 slices. Carefully push a stick into each slice, then place them on a baking tray lined with baking paper and pop them into the freezer for 20 minutes.

2 Melt the chocolate by putting it into a small heatproof bowl over a pan of simmering water, ensuring the base of the bowl doesn't touch the water. Alternatively melt it in the microwave on a low setting. Allow it to cool slightly.

3 Dip the bananas into the chocolate and leave to set. Chop into pieces if necessary.

easy baked pears

A delicious way of encouraging your little ones to eat nutritious pears.

8+ MONTHS

makes 8 toddler or 2 adult and 4 toddler portions

4 evenly sized pears (such as Conference, Comice, William)

juice of 2 oranges

1 Preheat the oven to 190°C/375°F/gas mark 5. Peel, quarter and core the pears. Scatter them in a snug layer in a roasting tray or ovenproof dish and drizzle over the orange juice. (If you don't have any oranges, you can use 3–4 tablespoons of ready-squeezed orange juice – you want to provide a little bit of moisture to help the pears steam as well as caramelize).

2 Bake the pears for about 30–40 minutes, depending on their ripeness, until soft and golden. Mash or chop if necessary. You can eat them warm with custard or porridge, or cool with yoghurt. They are also delicious mashed on a slice of lightly buttered wholemeal toast.

baked apples

A real family favourite!

9+ MONTHS

makes 6 baby or 2 adult and 2 baby portions

50g/2oz sultanas

50g/2oz dried unsulphured apricots, finely chopped

25g/1oz currants

25g/1oz dried figs, stalks removed, finely chopped

1 tablespoon apple and pear pure fruit spread

2 tablespoons fresh orange juice

2 tablespoons dried coconut shavings (optional)

4 medium-sized Bramley, or other type of cooking apples

1 Put all the ingredients except the apples into a mixing bowl. Stir together and leave for about 20 minutes to let the flavours blend. Preheat the oven to 180°C/350°F/gas mark 4.

2 Wash the apples well and cut them in half width-wise. Remove the core, using either a melon baller or a small sharp knife, and place the apple halves on a baking sheet, skin downwards. Stuff the filling into the middle of the apples – the mixture will also spread out on to the top, which is fine. Cover with foil and bake on the middle shelf of the oven for 25–30 minutes, until the apples are soft.

3 Serve, mashed or chopped up if necessary, with custard, natural yoghurt or ice cream.

banana and walnut loaf cake

This is one of the tastiest and most nutritious cakes I can think of.

12+ MONTHS

makes 1 cake

4 medium bananas

1 teaspoon ground cinnamon

1 rounded teaspoon baking powder

110g/3¾oz plain white flour

110g/3¾oz wholemeal flour

grated zest of 1 orange and 1 lemon

110g/3¾oz softened butter, cut into cubes

175g/6oz soft dark brown sugar

2 large eggs, lightly beaten

110g/3¾oz chopped dried ready-to-eat figs

50g/2oz medjool dates, stoned and chopped

175g/6oz walnut pieces, roughly chopped (not suitable for those with a family history of allergy, see page 208)

1 Preheat the oven to 180°C/350°F/gas mark 4. Lightly butter a 1kg/2lb 4oz loaf tin and line the base and ends with strips of baking parchment.

2 Peel the bananas, put them into a small bowl, and mash to a purée with a fork. Put the cinnamon and baking powder into a large mixing bowl and sieve both the flours on top, finally tipping in the bran that's left over in the sieve. Add the orange and lemon zest, butter, sugar and eggs and mix everything together thoroughly, ideally using an electric hand whisk. When the mixture is smooth, add the dried fruit and walnuts and stir them in.

3 Pop the mixture into the prepared tin, spread it level and bake in the middle of the oven for about 1¼-1½ hours, or until a skewer inserted into the loaf comes out clean. Allow to cool before slicing and, if you like, spreading with a little butter.

fruit bars

Ideal for the lunchbox of a toddler at nursery.

makes 24 fruit bars

175g/6oz unsalted butter

75g/2½oz honey (not suitable for children under 12 months)

50g/2oz pear and prune pure fruit spread

125g/4½oz demerara sugar

250g/9oz jumbo porridge oats

75g/2½oz pecan nut halves, roughly chopped (not suitable for children with a family history of allergies, see page 208)

75g/2½oz dried unsulphured apricots, finely chopped

75g/2½oz dried stoned dates, chopped

25g/1oz dried cranberries

75g/2½oz sultanas

75g/2½oz dried figs, tough stalks removed and chopped

25g/1oz each of pumpkin and sunflower seeds (see above)

25g/1oz unsalted pistachios, roughly chopped (see above)

25g/1oz linseeds (see above)

50g/2oz ground almonds (see above)

25g/1oz shaved coconut

1 Preheat the oven to 190°C/375°F/gas mark 5 and line a 23cm/9 inch square baking tin with greaseproof paper.

2 Melt the butter in a large saucepan, add the honey, pure fruit spread and sugar and stir gently for about a minute, until the sugar dissolves. Bring to the boil and simmer for a couple of minutes, stirring all the time.

3 Remove from the heat and add all the remaining ingredients. Mix well and pour into the baking tin. Spread the mixture out evenly. Bake until golden brown (approximately 20 minutes).

4 Leave to cool for about 10 minutes, then mark into bars and remove from the tin to cool completely. Chop into small pieces if necessary.

raspberry and apple muffins

These are a real treat for breakfast and a teatime favourite.

makes 24 muffins

25g/1oz very soft unsalted butter

4 tablespoons runny honey (not suitable for children under 12 months)

3 large eggs, beaten

50ml/2fl oz milk

50ml/2fl oz sunflower oil

250g/9oz wholemeal flour

250g/9oz plain white flour

2 teaspoons baking powder

2 teaspoons mixed spice

a large handful of crushed cornflakes

2 eating apples, coarsely grated but not peeled

200g/7oz raspberries

2 ripe bananas, mashed

juice of 1 orange

1 Preheat the oven to 180°C/350°F/gas mark 4 and line two 12-hole muffin tins with paper muffin cases.

2 In a large bowl mix together the butter and honey. Add the eggs, milk and oil and beat together until you have a well-mixed liquid.

3 In another bowl sieve together the flours, baking powder and spice. Add the cornflakes and mix well.

4 Gently fold the dry ingredients into the egg mixture with a metal spoon, trying to get as much air into the mixture as possible. Throw in the apples, raspberries, bananas and orange juice and mix gently. Spoon the mixture into the paper cases and bake for about 30 minutes, until golden brown, swapping the trays over halfway through.

sticky fig and apple cake with orange frosting

The combination of dried and fresh fruits make this deliciously nutritious.

10+
MONTHS

makes 24 muffins

300g/10½oz wholemeal flour

2 teaspoons baking powder

2 teaspoons ground cinnamon

1 teaspoon mixed spice

175ml/6fl oz olive oil

150ml/5½fl oz apple concentrate

2 large eggs, lightly beaten

3 tablespoons maple syrup

150g/5½oz peeled and grated Bramley apple

100g/3½oz grated carrot

2 handfuls (about 175g/6oz) of chopped dried figs

3 tablespoons apple and pear pure fruit spread

FOR THE FROSTING

250g/9oz mascarpone cheese

2 tablespoons natural full cream yoghurt

2 tablespoons maple syrup

1 teaspoon vanilla essence

zest of ½ an orange

1 Preheat the oven to 180°C/350°F/gas mark 4. Grease a 20cm/8 inch round springform cake tin and line the base with baking paper.

2 Sieve the flour, baking powder and spices together in a large bowl. Whisk the olive oil, apple concentrate, eggs and maple syrup together in another bowl.

3 Add the oily mixture to the flour and spice bowl and stir well, trying to lift lots of air into the mixture.

4 Add the apple, carrot and figs and gently fold until lightly mixed; don't beat, as this will make the cake heavy.

5 Spoon the mixture into the prepared cake tin and bake for 1 hour 20 minutes – it's cooked when a skewer comes out clean. Remove from the oven and allow to cool.

6 To make the frosting, mix the ingredients together. When the cake is cool, slice it crossways into two layers. Spread the bottom layer with the fruit spread and half the frosting. Place the other cake layer on top and decorate with the remaining frosting.

maya's birthday cake

12+
MONTHS

This birthday cake started off as a real disaster (why is it that I can make the deepest sponge cakes when there is no pressure, yet when I really want them to be great, they flop!). So I rescued it with the filling and the topping and everyone thought it was all intentionally delicious.

makes 1 20cm/8 inch cake

175g/6oz very soft butter

175g/6oz caster sugar

3 large eggs, beaten

½ teaspoon vanilla extract

175g/6oz self-raising flour

1 rounded teaspoon baking powder

a little milk (optional)

4 tablespoons blackcurrant or raspberry pure fruit spread

250g/9oz raspberries

FOR THE ICING

250g/9oz mascarpone cheese

200ml/7fl oz natural full-cream yoghurt

1 tablespoon maple syrup

1 teaspoon vanilla essence

1 Preheat the oven to 170°C/325°F/ gas mark 3. You will need two 20cm x 4cm/8 inch x 1½ inch deep non-stick sponge tins, lightly buttered and the bases lined with discs of baking parchment.

2 Beat together the butter and sugar until light and soft – the mixture will turn creamy and fluffy. Add a little of the egg at a time, mixing well after each addition to prevent curdling (if it does curdle, just add a tablespoon of the flour mixture and this will stop it). Continue until all the egg is added. Then add the vanilla extract.

3 Meanwhile, sieve the flour and baking powder into a large mixing bowl or on to a sheet of baking parchment, holding the sieve high to give it a good airing.

4 Fold the flour into the butter and sugar mixture gradually until it is all incorporated. What you should now have is a mixture that will drop off a spoon when you give it a tap on the side of the bowl. If it seems too stiff, add a little milk and mix again.

5 Divide the mixture between the two tins, level it out, and bake on the centre shelf of the oven for 15–20 minutes. Don't open the oven door until 15 minutes have elapsed. The cakes should be golden and slightly shrunken away from the sides of the tins. To test whether they're cooked or not, touch the centre of each lightly with a

finger; if it leaves no impression and the sponges spring back, they're ready. Remove them from the oven and leave in the tins for about 5 minutes before turning them out on to a wire cooling rack.

6 Traditionally you would leave the cakes to cool, but I didn't do that because I was in a rush (and actually it made the cake even more tasty not to wait). So, while still warm, spread 2 tablespoons of pure fruit spread over the surface of each cake – I used blackcurrant, which added a nice tang to the cake, but you could also use raspberry. Scatter a third of the raspberries over one of the cakes, top with the other cake, fruit spread side down, and press gently together. Leave to cool.

7 To make the filling, mix the mascarpone, yoghurt, maple syrup and vanilla, using a balloon whisk, which is the quickest way to blend them all together and to slightly thicken the mixture. Lightly mash the raspberries to get rid of any big pieces, then stir them into the icing. Separate the cakes again, pop half the icing inside and spread level. Put the cakes back together and spread the remaining icing on top.

8 You could leave the cake plain, with a ribbon round it, but a real party winner is to frost some edible flowers, such as violets. This is easy: in a small bowl whisk up an egg white until frothy. Cover a small plate with caster sugar, then very gently dip the flowers first into the egg white and then into the sugar until they're lightly coated in crystals. Leave to set for an hour, before popping on top of the cake. These sugar-frosted edible flowers will last for about 4 days if you store them in a cool dark place.

food and wellbeing

In this chapter, I'll show you how you can help babies and toddlers deal with many of the common childhood ailments and conditions, from teething pain, constipation and diarrhoea, to coughs and colds, and carrying too much weight. The foods you give your child can help his body fight infection and also help him to feel better in general.

Anyone who suspects their baby or toddler has a food intolerance should try keeping a food diary – it will help your doctor or dietitian to advise you well. If your child is ill, however, or suffers a severe allergic reaction, you should seek advice from your GP immediately.

To keep a food diary, you need to write down everything your child eats and drinks for a fortnight – what he ate, the date and time he ate it, how much he ate and any symptoms that followed; ideally, it is also helpful to note the date and time each symptom appeared, although this may not be possible and isn't essential. Ask any carers at your child's playgroup or nursery to do the same.

energy and concentration

low energy

'Tired all the time' is probably how most new parents, and indeed seasoned ones, would describe themselves. But on a great day, when everything goes well, we can feel energetic and like we can do it all. Just as we parents go through peaks and troughs with our energy levels, our babies and toddlers will do the same.

YOUR BABY'S FIRST YEAR

In your baby's first year tiredness is hopefully not an issue, as his sleeping and feeding routine should sustain him. But if you're worried by his lethargy, seek medical advice, especially if he's not putting on weight or being as alert as the pictures in your baby books or your friends' babies lead you to believe he should be. It may be that you need to look at how nutritious the milk you're feeding him is – and possibly supplement it with more, or a different, feed.

12 MONTHS +

If you notice the energy levels of a child over 1 year old flagging consistently, or if staff at the nursery report that he seems to be struggling with keeping going and staying awake, consider the following possibilities. There are several nutritional things you can try to give him more *joie de vivre*.

DEHYDRATION

Many toddlers don't drink enough water – particularly in the summer or when they've eaten a sugary or salty snack. Tiredness can be one symptom of this. Other symptoms are dark-coloured urine (it should be very pale), thirst, headaches and finding exercise difficult.

APPETITE

If a toddler is eating too little or too much he's likely to get tired. Remember that if he's going through a growth spurt he may need more nutritious 'pit-stop' snacks to keep his energy levels up. Make sure his diet is varied and that he has regular meals. Too many high-GI

LOW ENERGY MEDICINE CHEST

- Do ensure he eats regular meals
- Do ensure he eats enough
- Do ensure he doesn't eat too much
- Do ensure he drinks enough water
- Do ask your GP to test for anaemia if your child consistently seems to lack energy

sweet foods or juices can send his sugar and energy levels up and down. Too much fibre may mean he gets too little energy from his diet. Toddlers over 1 year up to the age of 3 should have roughly one-third wholegrain to two-thirds more refined, such as white rice, white pasta, bread, etc.

ANAEMIA

Anaemia is lack of haemoglobin, which carries oxygen in the blood around the body. The most common type of anaemia is caused by too little iron in the diet (hence it's medical name – iron-deficiency anaemia). One of the reasons we start weaning at 6 months is to introduce more iron into babies' diets, as milk no longer meets their high iron requirements. If your toddler looks pale or is constantly tired, or if he suffers from headaches, dizziness, shortness of breath, frequent crying or poor memory, or if he often gets colds or other infections, it's possible that he has iron-deficiency anaemia. If you suspect this might be the case, you should see your GP, who can test for the condition. If your child tests positive for iron-deficiency anaemia, you will need to focus on boosting his intake of foods rich in iron and vitamin C (see page 77).

DIABETES

You should also see your GP if, as well as being tired, your child displays some of the following signs, as he may need a test for diabetes: increased thirst, suspected blurred vision, always having to wee, and feeling or looking excessively tired.

COELIAC DISEASE

If you are sure none of the above is the cause of your child's tiredness, another possibility is that he may have coeliac disease. It's especially important to consider this if you have this autoimmune disease in your family or notice that your children have problems digesting gluten and have fatty, foul-smelling stools (see page 207). However, it's important to seek the advice of your GP before cutting gluten out of your child's diet, as this can delay finding out if coeliac disease actually is the cause of his tiredness.

EXERCISE AND EMOTIONS

Check that your child is getting enough exercise. As with adults, lack of fresh air and good old running around in the park can make toddlers feel tired. Of course, the reason for his tiredness may be nothing nutritional or physical, more an emotional thing, such as starting a new playgroup, or having worries about an unhappy home environment. Reassuring him and restoring his confidence are the best things you can do.

boosting learning power

Although babyhood is a bit early to expect your child to be a little Einstein, we all want to help our children do well, and one way to encourage this is to provide his brain with the right foods.

Both breast milk and formula provide babies with all the nutrition they need up to the age of 6 months. But once weaning has taken hold, at 7 months, you need to consider the following.

If your baby or toddler suffers from poor concentration, think about whether he is getting enough essential brain nutrients such as iron and the B vitamins (especially if you're bringing him up as a vegetarian or vegan or if he's a fussy eater). B vitamins are found in red meat, chicken, eggs, wholegrain cereals, brown rice, green leafy vegetables, cheese, yoghurt and milk. If you have a vegetarian or vegan child and you want to check that he's getting the right balance of nutrients, see pages 80–81.

WATER

I believe water reduces tiredness and enables concentration. All babies, apart from those pre-weaning babies who are fed exclusively on milk, need to drink water. Offer weaning babies boiled and cooled water regularly – at least at all meals and snack times plus mid-morning and mid-afternoon. Remember not to reboil water, as it concentrates the minerals. Once they reach 12 months water no longer needs to be boiled.

Toddlers who are active should drink 6–8 small glasses of water a day.

BREAKFAST

A good breakfast is very important. It can significantly boost concentration and memory, and help babies and toddlers to be more creative and energetic.

As soon as your baby is old enough, it's best to go for the complex carbohydrates (see pages 70–71). These will make him feel full for longer, and that means his energy levels, moods and concentration, will be much steadier. A fresh fruit smoothie (diluted with water, as they're a little too strong neat) that contains yoghurt is a great breakfast for 7-months plus. Sugary cereals give them a kick to start off with, but can leave them frazzled and unable to sit still afterwards.

BOOSTING LEARNING POWER MEDICINE CHEST

- **Do ensure he gets enough iron**
- **Do ensure he gets enough B vitamins**
- **Do ensure he gets enough omega-3**
- **Do ensure he drinks enough water**
- **Do ensure he eats a good breakfast**

- **Don't feed him high-sugar foods**

BLOOD SUGAR LEVELS

Like all your family, your baby's day should be based around fresh fruits and vegetables and lean proteins. Whole grains are also important, but limit them in babies under 1 year. Try to stick to foods with a low glycaemic index (GI) value, which won't send your child's blood sugar levels first sky-high and then crashing down – rapid sugar swings do seem to affect their brain-power. Ask the carers at your child's playgroup or nursery not to serve sweet drinks and sweet biscuits – water and fruit are much healthier.

GOOD FATS

There is evidence that a diet rich in omega-3 fatty acids can help develop a child's brain-power. There seems to be a craze for giving our children omega-3 supplements in the hope of turning them into geniuses. But remember, omega-3 is only one aspect of optimizing your child's intelligence/behaviour – a balanced, nourishing diet can have just as profound an effect.

From 7 months, the best sources of omega-3 fatty acids are oily fish: sardines, fresh tuna, mackerel, herrings (although limit the oily-fish intake to one to two 80g portions a week as there are concerns over mercury levels). Salmon fishcakes, fish pie (page 134), sardines on toast, pitta bread with one of my fish pâtés (page 135), fresh tuna and rice – all the family can benefit from such nourishing meals once your baby is ready for the texture. You can also get useful omega-3 fats from sunflower and hemp seeds and other nuts and seeds (these can be eaten ground up from 7 months, but should be avoided if there is any family history of allergies).

E NUMBERS AND CAFFEINE

Research shows that excessive intake of E numbers such as tartrazine, or indeed caffeine, can lead to poor concentration – so try to keep them out of your baby or toddler's diet. Caffeine stops toddlers sleeping properly – avoid cola or any other caffeine-rich drink, even chocolate, which contains a similar substance (so keep hot chocolate well diluted).

'Your baby's day should be based around fresh fruits and vegetables and lean proteins.'

constantly hungry

Even small babies can go through feast and famine days. It's not necessarily a problem, so don't worry too much.

BABIES UNDER 6 MONTHS

Being hungry all the time may simply mean that your baby is having a growth spurt – babies typically go through growth spurts at 2, 3 and 6 months. In this case he should be having larger milk feeds. But occasionally babies 'comfort suck' and appear to be demanding milk, when actually they just want a cuddle – in time you'll be able to work out your baby's different cries and needs.

If the hunger seems to be a continual issue, discuss with your health visitor and doctor whether you need to change to a casein-based feed, specifically designed for hungrier babies (see page 30).

BREAST-FEEDING

If you're breast-feeding and your baby's constantly hungry, keep a check on how well you're eating and whether your baby's been gaining much weight recently; is your health visitor happy with his weight gain? It may be that your milk is not satisfying enough, in which case try to eat more and rest more.

If your breast milk doesn't appear to be satisfying your baby, you may need to supplement it with bottle feeds, so discuss this with your health visitor. Bear in mind, though, that sometimes your baby may start to prefer the bottle teat, which could make him more reluctant to take your breast, possibly reducing your milk supply.

READY TO WEAN?

Depending on your baby's age, perpetual hunger may be a sign that he's ready to start eating some solids, but this should only be considered when he's at least

CONSTANTLY HUNGRY MEDICINE CHEST

- **Do feed him more if he's going through a growth spurt**
- **Do – if he's over 4 months – consider weaning or moving to the next stage of weaning**
- **Do ensure weaning and weaned babies drink enough water**
- **Do ensure he doesn't rush his food**
- **Do – if he's weaned or weaning – ensure he eats a balanced diet**

- **Don't wean before 4 months**
- **Don't give sugary snacks**

4 months old. Before this time, babies' bodies, especially their kidneys, aren't physiologically able to deal with food, and it's more difficult for their gastric juices to digest the protein. Also, neurologically, their co-ordination isn't well enough developed to maintain the right posture to be able to swallow food. If your baby is 4 months or over, you can discuss the option of introducing some solids with your health visitor – but in many ways it's best to wait until he's 6 months. Don't start introducing things like rusk in his milk bottle, as there's the possibility he could choke.

WEANING BABIES

Hunger may just be a signal that your baby is ready to get his 'teeth' into something more solid and substantial – bread and pasta, say, rather than a vegetable or fruit purée. For a 7-month-plus baby, adding extra fat to purées, in the form of custard, full cream yoghurt, butter or olive oil, ricotta or some other cheese, will keep him satisfied for longer. Watch that you're giving your baby enough fats and full cream ingredients such as yoghurt, especially if you're bringing him up as a vegetarian or vegan, as sometimes these babies may be hungry because they're getting enough fruits and veggies, but not enough calories (see pages 80–81).

WEANING BABIES AND TODDLERS

Check that they're not dehydrated, as they may interpret this as hunger. Hunger may also be a symptom of a growth spurt – try giving him larger nutritious meals and good snacks.

Think about whether he has just been through a stage of not being bothered about food. If so, help him catch up by giving him bigger portions and good snacks. It's important, though, to stick to a routine, otherwise he could start thinking he can have food whenever he likes, potentially leading to problems in the future.

TODDLERS

With a toddler, if you think that he's getting enough physical nourishment, ask yourself whether it might be boredom or comfort eating. If so, try to find out the reason: perhaps he's feeling insecure about something.

If he's rushing his food, try to get him to eat slowly, as this gives more time for his body to recognize when he's eaten enough. And make sure his meals have a good balance of carbohydrates, proteins and good fats.

Alarmingly, the UK has the second highest incidence of obesity in northern and western Europe, after Germany. And the situation seems to be getting worse – we only need to look in playgrounds and swimming pools to see how many children are carrying far too much fat. It's serious now.

So if you're worried about your child's weight, you're not alone – the latest statistics say that one-third of our kids are now too fat, with over a million children in this country being clinically overweight. However, when your child is a toddler you have the power to influence his eating patterns. Other people's influences don't come into play so much. So be strong and crack the weight issue in the right way now, before it becomes a bigger problem.

BABIES AND WEIGHT

During the first 12 months of your baby's life, your health visitor will help you keep an eye on how much weight he is putting on. It's very rare for babies under 12 months to be overweight, as physically they can only drink a certain amount of milk. Their stomachs are so small and their energy requirements for growth are so high that they usually can't consume too many calories. And at this age they don't have the skills and will to demand more food.

Remember that a crying baby doesn't necessarily need more food – babies cry for many different reasons. Sometimes they can be thirsty, in which case water can be a good thirst-quencher, rather than extra milk.

TODDLERS AND WEIGHT

It's usually when children are aged 2 or older that they can become more prone to being overweight if they are fairly sedentary and their diet is unbalanced. Of course when they're toddlers with strong wills and a pair of powerful lungs, it's easy to fall into the trap of giving them something to eat or drink every time they ask, and this may well be where needless calories come in.

If your toddler is technically overweight, your goal should normally be to maintain him at a static weight so

TODDLER WEIGHT AND OBESITY MEDICINE CHEST

- **Do look at your mealtime routines**
- **Do cut down on fats and sugars**
- **Do encourage him to eat more slowly**
- **Do encourage wholegrains (limit these for a baby under 12 months)**
- **Do give him more water**
- **Do introduce more exercise**
- **Do consult a doctor if he is obese**

- **Don't encourage your child to eat 'low-fat' products**
- **Don't put your toddler on the scales regularly unless he is obese**

that he becomes much leaner as he grows taller. However, I don't recommend that you regularly weigh toddlers unless they're obese. It can lead to weight obsession and is often unrealistic because of toddlers' growth spurts. Just use your eyes, and their clothes, as a check that they're heading in the right direction.

OBESITY

If your toddler is obese, your doctor may suggest he loses some weight because being much too heavy could compromise his mobility and development. Parents of an obese toddler should seek professional support from a paediatric dietitian before making any changes, as they will need to ensure that he's losing weight healthily. Your GP will refer to you a suitable dietitian – they can be incredibly supportive, and it's also good to share the responsibility with a professional outsider.

IS YOUR TODDLER TOO HEAVY?

To find out if your toddler is technically overweight, look at his percentile charts and see if his weight centile is much higher than his height centile (for example, if he's on the 95th centile for weight and only the 50th centile for height, this means he's overweight).

Body mass index (BMI) is another useful measure. You can work out his BMI as follows. Measure his height in metres and square this figure (multiply it by itself). For example, if his height is 0.9m you multiply 0.9 by 0.9 = $0.81m^2$. Then write down his weight in kilograms (kg). Divide the weight (in kg) by the square of the height (in m^2) and this will give you the BMI.

You may find charts that give slightly different figures, and it also depends on how muscly or fat your child is, but here's the way I work out how big the problem is. A 2-year old boy is overweight if his BMI is 18.4 or over; a girl at 18 or over. A 3-year old boy is overweight if his BMI is 17.9 or over; a girl at 17.6 or over.

WHAT TO DO

Excess weight and obesity are complex areas. There are a few things that I have found really help toddlers stop putting on too much weight. Don't try to do everything listed here straight away, just look on the next few weeks as a time to see what you can do to make family eating, and therefore your toddler's eating, as healthy as possible.

It's miserable being an overweight toddler – children as young as 3 can be bullied or feel excluded from activities because they're chunky or can't run fast. Of course there are also all the health issues – the first signs of heart disease have been found in children as young as 7 or 8, and an overweight 3-year-old can already be on the way down this path.

EMOTIONAL ISSUES

Before making changes to your toddler's diet or exercise, consider why he might be putting on weight. Has something changed at home? Perhaps he's seeing less of one parent or the other – could he be overeating for comfort reasons?

EATING ROUTINE

Think about your routine – you may be cooking more fried or creamy foods and sugary puddings than you think. Keeping a family diary for a few days can show you in black and white what you're all eating. Are you having more ready-made meals or fast foods than usual? Is your child nibbling crisps and chocolates while watching TV?

Also think about whether you're giving your toddler too many treats. Don't pack snacks for short journeys and give water instead of sweet drinks whenever possible.

THREE MEALS A DAY

Structure the day around 3 meals, ideally with the whole family eating together at fairly regular times. Otherwise, if you push their hunger too far, they'll ask for snacks and be too full to eat a nutritious meal later. On days when the meal plan goes awry, give them a healthy snack – fruit, raw vegetables or cheese.

EXERCISE

It's unrealistic to expect children to lose excess weight just by healthy eating – they need to burn up calories too. Exercise helps them feel confident and secure in their body, produces endorphins that can help to keep them happy, burns off anxiety and bad moods, pushes oxygen around their body, and tires them out! Get your toddler walking. Tricycles or little pushchairs they can push in the park can help. Walk with them around town, take them swimming, play ball games with them, or get them dancing.

HOW TO CUT DOWN YOUR TODDLER'S CALORIE INTAKE

- Serve smaller portions and put them on smaller plates.
- Don't insist he finishes everything.
- Encourage him to eat slowly and allow a short gap between the main course and any dessert.
- Don't give a dessert at every meal.
- Make sure he drinks enough water and limit juices.
- Use vegetables and fresh fruit to fill toddlers up. Steamed vegetables retain more goodness, but if he doesn't like them this way, try roasting them with a little olive oil.
- Change his milk to semi-skimmed after he's 2 (but don't shift to skimmed milk).
- Give him wholegrains – wholemeal toast, porridge, higher-fibre breakfast cereals, brown rice and wholemeal pasta, and keep the skins on potatoes.
- Keep proteins as lean as possible (meat, fish, eggs, chicken, seafood, etc.)
- Minimize unnecessary fats and sugars (keep a stock of foods he can eat freely, such as fresh fruit).
- Go for a variety of colours, tastes and textures in any one meal. The more variety he has in one meal, the more likely his brain is to register that he's eaten enough.
- Make healthy food look and taste good.
- Try to eat healthily as a family – your toddler will copy you.

constipation

All babies have days when they poo more than others. He may go four times a day, or once every couple of days, or anything in between – and of course what one parent thinks is constipation can be what another calls normal. Constipation is rare in babies, especially breast-fed ones, although it can become a problem when they start solid food. It's worth bearing in mind that all babies have to strain to some degree to pass a stool, even if it's soft or liquid.

You only need to take action if your baby or toddler poos less than once every three to four days, or if his poos are hard enough to cause him discomfort. You shouldn't worry about constipation (unless there are other signs of illness) – a baby's body, like an adult's, deals with food erratically.

Childhood constipation is caused by an abnormal amount of waste matter building up in the lower bowel, which becomes so hard that the baby or toddler is either unable, or afraid, to pass it, with the result that the waste becomes more compacted, making matters worse.

SYMPTOMS: BABIES UNDER 3 MONTHS

If your baby is newborn and passes less than one stool a day, this is usually regarded as constipation. For babies up to 3 months, constipation is rare, even when they are formula-fed. Some grunting is normal, but if your baby cries or looks uncomfortable, check with your GP or health visitor.

SYMPTOMS: 3 MONTHS +

For an older baby, especially one who has started solid food, symptoms to look out for are tummy-ache (which perhaps gets better after the bowels are opened), a distended or hard tummy, blood-streaked stools, or the classic hard rabbit pellets.

If your baby or toddler is passing blood, or has any other symptoms that worry you, consult your GP. A mild laxative may be necessary, but in most cases making dietary tweaks can help kick-start the gut (see remedies below). Be patient – if you get stressed out it will

TODDLER CONSTIPATION MEDICINE CHEST

- **Do ensure he drinks plenty of water**
- **Do give him lots of fruit and veg**
- **Do massage your baby or toddler**

- **Don't give too much rice or bananas, as these can be binding**

only make him more anxious, which in turn can make his body clamp up.

CAUSES

New foods or a minor illness can cause constipation. It can also be caused by emotional factors, such as if a parent hasn't been around much. Sometimes it can just be due to not drinking enough water.

Zealous potty training can lead to constipation, so don't put your toddler under too much pressure to use the potty and ensure you're not doing it too early. Try to be positive – introduce a reward for toilet 'successes' each time he passes a stool until he is fully potty trained.

A food intolerance or allergy may be the problem (although this is much less common than any of the above). If your child regularly has the same reaction to a food, reduce his intake. If the problem still doesn't go away, ask your GP to refer you to a paediatric dietitian.

WATER AS A REMEDY

Lack of fluid is one of the most common causes of constipation. Give babies cooled boiled water. Toddlers, too, should drink plenty of water. Chamomile or fennel tea, warm or cooled, is soothing for a constipated gut for weaned babies.

FRUIT AND VEG AS A REMEDY

Fruit, vegetables and wholegrains provide plenty of fibre, which is important for keeping the bowel moving (limit whole-grains in babies under 12 months). If it helps, try disguising veg in stews or pasta sauces or make purées and dips.

Fruits that seem to have a strong laxative effect include figs, dates, apricots, papayas, rhubarb and plums. Try giving a baby over 6 months a couple of teaspoons of fruit purée made from these fruits. To make a dried fruit purée (for babies over 7 months), cook the dried fruits in a little orange juice or water for about 20 minutes, then purée or mash with a fork. Mix with porridge, rice, yoghurt, or add to a fresh fruit smoothie. Date syrup is available from www.meridianfoods.co.uk – it's sweet, so only use a smidge. Bananas can bind, so you may want to cut down on them.

ALOE VERA AS A CURE

For babies over 12 months you can use good-quality aloe vera juice for constipation. It's bitter on its own, so mix it with fresh juice or water. Follow the dosage recommended on the bottle. Buy a juice derived from aloe vera gel, not from aloe latex, as the latter can be too potent for children. The juice should contain at least 98 per cent aloe vera and should not have any aloin or aloe-emoin compounds. Look for the 'IASC-certified' seal.

MASSAGE

Try bicycling your baby's legs if he seems constipated – it may help move stools along his intestine. Massaging babies' feet gently with either a base massage oil or a blend (6 drops patchouli, 4 drops geranium, 15 drops mandarin, diluted in 100ml vegetable base oil) can get things going, as can rubbing the tummy clockwise, starting at the lower left-hand side by the groin.

eczema

About one child in 20 develops a form of eczema called atopic eczema. It's heartbreaking to see children clawing away at their raw, itchy skin, making it worse. Of course, eczema varies greatly in severity – some children have a small patch; others are covered in it.

ECZEMA ROUND A BABY'S MOUTH

Too much lip-licking or thumb-sucking can cause a red rash around the mouth known as 'lick eczema'. This happens because saliva irritates the lips, making them chapped and dry. The best solution is to moisturize your baby's lips and protect the skin around his mouth with a barrier cream such as petroleum jelly, or a cream with comfrey or chamomile in it, which can soothe as well as protect. As soon as the habit stops, the eczema will heal.

THE AGE ECZEMA APPEARS

Eczema usually starts before a baby is 18 months, but it can develop later, especially if a toddler has an hay fever, asthma or any other allergic-type condition. Most children with atopic eczema grow out of it by their fourth birthday. If they develop it when they're older than 4 they can be affected until they're in their teens.

THE CAUSES OF ECZEMA

Eczema is an inflammatory condition that causes dry, itchy skin. If the skin is scratched, it can break and bleed, leading to infection. It's thought to be an allergic condition in which the body overreacts to something and produces too much Immunoglobulin G (also called IgG) or Immunoglobulin E (IgE) antibodies. Genes play a part, but environment, lifestyle and diet can all have an impact.

YOUR DIET DURING PREGNANCY

During your pregnancy, eating plenty of vitamin E reduces the chance of your baby having an allergy (see page 76 for good sources). It's also wise to avoid the most common food allergens (see page 203) and refined peanut oil, especially if you have a history of eczema or allergic conditions associated with those foods. Taking a probiotic lactobacillus supplement (see page 85) may reduce the chance of your baby suffering from eczema, but the evidence isn't conclusive.

ECZEMA MEDICINE CHEST

- **Do avoid the most common food allergens when pregnant**
- **Do eat plenty of foods rich in vitamin E when pregnant**
- **Do breast-feed your baby**
- **Do give older babies and toddlers foods rich in omega-3**
- **Do give older babies and toddlers foods rich in vitamin C**
- **Do keep a food diary to identify the allergen; show the diary to a paediatric dietitian or your doctor**
- **Do consider probiotics**

BREAST-FEEDING AND ECZEMA

There is strong evidence that breast-feeding helps prevent allergic disease. This is partly because foods such as cow's milk or cow's-milk formula, which may trigger the allergic process, are introduced later. But it is also because specific agents in breast milk may have protective potential. Eating foods rich in vitamin C when breast-feeding can also help reduce the risk.

Breast-fed babies who suffer from eczema may be sensitive to a food you are eating. Keep a food and symptom diary, detailing what you ate and how much at each time during each day, any symptoms seen and, ideally, when they appeared. But remember, you do need to ensure that your baby is still getting nutrient-rich milk, and that you're getting a plentiful diet yourself as well. So before cutting out any foods, I suggest you show the food diary to a health professional and discuss options.

FORMULA MILK AND ECZEMA

If your baby is formula-fed, talk to your GP or health visitor about whether you'd be better off using a soya-based formula, as the cow's-milk protein in conventional feeds may be the trigger for the eczema.

ECZEMA IN BABIES OVER 6 MONTHS

Above 6 months, there are things you can do to reduce the likelihood of a flare-up. Oily fish and other foods rich in omega-3 fatty acids can help with the inflammatory aspects of eczema (but limit the amount of oily fish due to concerns over mercury – see page 75). Or give him an omega oil supplement. It can take several weeks for the eczema to improve; once it has done so, you need to carry on giving the supplement.

Feed weaning babies lots of fresh fruit and vegetable purées (apart from citrus fruits, especially oranges, as they can irritate eczema) and chunks of fresh fruit and veg for older babies and toddlers. Use vegetable fats such as olive and hemp, flax or linseed oil, instead of butter and animal fats (the latter don't work well with the omega oils).

ALLERGEN FOODS

If you identify a food allergen and stop eating it while breast-feeding and avoid giving it to your baby as a food after 6 months, his skin can return virtually to normal. The most common food allergens are milk (usually cow's), eggs, citrus fruits, seeds, nuts, shellfish, wheat, soya and food additives.

Seek advice from a paediatric dietitian if your child has severe eczema and you suspect that a food allergy may be aggravating it. There are also non-food allergens, from household chemicals to soaps and shampoos to dust and mites.

OMEGA OIL SUPPLEMENTS

For babies over 6 months, the best omega-3 fatty acid is DHA (docosa-hexaenoic acid). The recommended dose is 100mg a day of DHA.

Omega-3 supplements must state that they're suitable for your child's age. They can be mixed into milk or juice.

food intolerance

Babies' immune systems are not strong, and can over-react to foods if they're given too early; this is one of the main reasons why we wait until 6 months to wean. By introducing small amounts of different foods at that stage we can help them develop an appropriate immune response and hopefully stop them becoming allergic.

ALLERGY CAUSES AND REACTIONS

A food allergy occurs when the immune system over-reacts to a particular food. The reactions, which are often immediate, include one or more of the following: swollen lips, an itchy mouth, vomiting, diarrhoea, hives, eczema, coughing, runny nose, wheezing and headache.

The most common food allergens in children are: cow's milk, nuts, eggs, soya milk and soya products (so don't automatically switch to soya milk), wheat, sesame seeds, fish and shellfish. But virtually any food or food additive can cause a reaction. Sometimes children can tolerate a food when it's cooked but not raw.

JUDGING THE ALLERGY RISK

If your child has suffered a bad allergic reaction to food in the past, it might happen again and might be more severe. If he has asthma as well as allergies, ask for a referral to a paediatrician because this can put him into a higher-risk category. Mild reactions to foods should not be ignored because future reactions may be severe. If the doctor judges that your child is at risk of a severe reaction or anaphylaxis (see below), he may prescribe a pre-loaded junior adrenaline (epinephrine) injection for you to keep and then use if your child does have a severe reaction.

Be alert to your child's symptoms and take them seriously. Give the adrenaline injection if you think he's beginning to show signs of a severe reaction – don't wait until you are sure. Even if you give him adrenaline, the hospital needs to check him over as soon as possible. Make sure your family, friends, nursery, etc. know when and how to use the adrenaline.

ANAPHYLAXIS

Anaphylaxis is a life-threatening allergic reaction to a food or drink (or a drug or an insect bite). It can hit within seconds, or hours later. It is usually the result of a child eating the offending food, but it can result from just touching it. In anaphylaxis the blood vessels swell and the blood pressure drops. The lips and/or throat can swell, which can cause problems with breathing and talking. The heart can race; hives, rashes and red weals can appear; and the child can start wheezing. The lowered blood pressure can make children feel weak and even collapse. Immediately give the child a pre-loaded junior adrenaline (epinephrine) injection; it works quickly and he will soon return to normal.

FOOD INTOLERANCES

Food intolerances can cause digestive problems, rashes, headaches and unexplained fatigue.

milk intolerance

Some children fare better if they avoid cow's milk. This might be because they have a problem with cow's milk protein, or it might be because they are lactose-intolerant (lactose is the sugar in milk). Lactose-intolerance is caused by a lack of lactase, the enzyme that breaks down lactose, in your child's body.

If your child has an intolerance of cow's milk protein, he should still be able to tolerate other sorts of dairy milk, such as sheep's (although not always). But if he's lactose-intolerant, you need to go for cereal-based milks such as soya, oat, almond and rice milk.

If your baby's under 6 months, seek advice from your GP or health visitor if you suspect he isn't reacting well to milk. If there's a problem with cow's milk protein, the symptoms – diarrhoea, vomiting, not putting on weight – usually appear early, and the problem usually corrects itself and disappears by the time the child is 3 years old.

BREAST-FED BABIES AND LACTOSE INTOLERANCE

If you are breast-feeding and your baby becomes lactose-intolerant, the only thing you can do is change to one of the non-lactose-containing formulas, which are usually based on soya (but read the information on soya milk on pages 30-31). You should discuss this with your health visitor or doctor first, though, to make sure lactose intolerance is in fact the problem.

WHAT FOODS TO SUBSTITUTE FOR MILK PRODUCTS

Under 6 months

Your GP and health visitor will advise you about a suitable infant formula, which will probably be a special casein hydrolyzed formula such as Nutramigen or Pregestimil. These are made from cow's milk that has been treated to change the proteins. A few milk-allergic children still react to these and need an amino acid-based milk such as Neocate.

Over 6 months

When you drop a food group from your child's diet you should add a different source of the nutrients the dropped food provided. If milk is dropped, you will need to find another source of calcium.

Try the following:

- Fortified soya milks.
- At around 7 months you can introduce pulses, puréed or mashed green leafy vegetables and small-boned fish such as sardines.
- Try sheep's milk, cheese, yoghurt and butter (although since the milk proteins are very similar they could also cause a reaction).

Note: Some olive oil spreads are dairy-free (check the labels, but you also need to check that they don't contain hydrogenated fats or trans fatty acids, as these are bad for the heart).

Talk to your GP or dietitian about calcium supplements.

FORMULA-FED BABIES AND LACTOSE INTOLERANCE

If you are using the normal cow's-milk-based formula and your baby suffers from an intolerance, again it's important to discuss it before changing to a soya formula. Babies are sometimes intolerant of or allergic to soya (see pages 30-31), so you need professional support to ensure you're making the right choice.

BABIES 6 MONTHS + AND LACTOSE INTOLERANCE

With a baby over 6 months, before you cut anything out of his diet, keep a food diary for a couple of weeks, recording what and how much of it he eats and drinks, and noting his symptoms, just to be sure milk is the cause and not some other imbalance in his diet. If the food diary makes you think your baby has a milk intolerance, cut out dairy foods completely for a couple of weeks. This

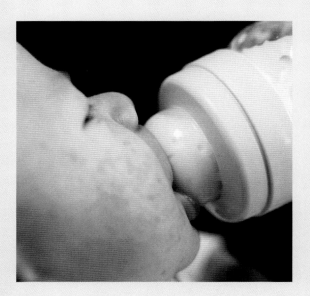

includes avoiding ghee, butter fat, buttermilk, butter oil, casein, whey, sodium caseinate and calcium caseinate. If, after a few weeks off dairy, he starts to feel much better, you could try giving him a little lactose (say some sheep's cheese or yoghurt) every couple of days to see if this triggers any symptoms. However, you should discuss this with a health professional.

wheat intolerance

Wheat and wheat-based foods such as pasta, pizza, bread, etc. are perfectly healthy for most babies over the age of 6 months to eat. However, if you suspect your baby suffers from wheat intolerance, keep a food diary. You could try taking obvious wheat foods out of his diet for a couple of weeks to see if the symptoms disappear or lessen significantly. However, I strongly suggest you only continue this with professional help and once a definite diagnosis has been made.

COELIAC DISEASE

If you notice that your baby has any of the following symptoms after eating wheat, you need to take him to your GP before you change his diet, because your baby might have coeliac disease: weight loss or failure to gain weight; stomach pains and rectal bleeding; very pale, floating stools that have an unpleasant smell; or pale skin and tiredness, which is due to lack of energy because your baby is anaemic.

food allergies

nut allergy

Peanut allergy is the most common nut allergy, frequently resulting in a very severe anaphylactic reaction. If there is a history of allergies (such as asthma, eczema, hay fever, food allergies) in your family, don't introduce nuts of any sort of sesame seeds or their products into your child's diet before the age of 3. (Whole nuts should not be given to children under the age of 5 because of the risk of choking.)

However, if you don't have a family history of allergy you can introduce small amounts of nuts, smooth nut butters, or nut oils, after the age of 7 months, as it seems that a small amount of exposure to nuts helps the immune system develop an appropriate reaction.

NUT ALLERGY – FOODS TO AVOID

Peanuts in particular

Other nuts that grow on trees, such as pecans, walnuts and hazelnuts

Seeds, particularly sesame seeds

Kernels, such as pine nuts

Note: Coconut is not a nut, so it doesn't have to be avoided

egg allergy

Egg allergy is one of the most common food allergies, and babies up to 12 months should only be given hard-boiled, well-cooked eggs. By 12 months, most babies' immune systems should be mature enough not to react badly.

EGG ALLERGY IN BABIES

Egg allergy is most common under 12 months and then becomes progressively less of a problem. Few children are allergic to egg after the age of 6 years, although in some cases an allergy can persist into adult life. Children with other allergies (such as cow's milk) or with a family history of allergy seem to be particularly vulnerable – so if this is the case, talk things through with your health visitor or GP.

More than half the babies who develop egg allergy begin to have symptoms within minutes of being given an egg for the first time. While it is possible that some have received small amounts of egg in a manufactured baby food, it is also possible that they have actually been sensitized before birth or via breast milk.

THE SIGNS OF EGG ALLERGY

The development of an egg allergy can be dramatic in babies, but rarely causes a severe anaphylactic reaction. A red rash usually appears around the mouth within seconds of eating an egg, followed a few minutes later by swelling around and inside the mouth and on the face. A few babies vomit, but loose stools are relatively uncommon. After a while, parts of the skin can swell, or they may develop eczema and/or wheezing, sneezing, or watery eyes. If you suspect that your baby has an allergy to eggs, seek professional advice.

EGG ALLERGIES AND MMR

The MMR (measles, mumps and rubella) injection is normally cultured using eggs. Anaphylactic reactions to the MMR have been reported, but they are very rare. However, if you have a child with a severe egg or any other food allergy you should let your GP know before any immunizations.

'Egg allergy is most common under 12 months and then becomes progressively less of a problem.'

EGG ALLERGY – FOODS TO AVOID

A paediatric dietitian will be able to help you through the long list of products you need to avoid. As well as 'egg'. look out for and avoid 'albumen' on food labels.

Note: Sometimes small quantities of egg in a cooked food may cause no reaction in a child with a mild egg allergy (in which case he's more likely to grow out of it) as heat can alter egg proteins.

• Look out for foods that may have a surprise egg content, such as some breads, the glazes on buns or pies, pastas, and sweets such as 'dolly mixture'! Although some pasta does contain egg, you can find plenty that doesn't and it tastes just as good.

• The emulsifier known as lecithin can be derived from egg, although in practice this is uncommon..

teething and toothache

Your baby will probably start cutting his first tooth any time between 6 and 12 months – sometimes it can be even later. The pain of teething can be excruciating. Although the first few milk teeth at the front usually creep through with relatively little discomfort, the pain can kick in big-time when the big molars and canines start coming through. All the primary teeth, otherwise known as the milk teeth, have usually emerged by the time children are 3 years old.

SIGNS OF TEETHING

The first tell-tale sign of your baby's teeth coming through can be dribbling, red cheeks and sore gums. Sometimes babies have a fever or diarrhoea, and sleep tends to be seriously disrupted. Your baby will just want to pop his fingers into his mouth, trying to soothe his gums – he may also become more clingy, always wanting to be carried, wingeing and crying more often.

TEETHING REMEDIES

Your baby's instinct – to put his fingers or something else, like a hard toy, in his mouth – is a good one. Chewing on something hard and cool, like a carrot stick or a piece of cucumber, can really help. You can buy teething rings that you keep in the fridge, making them comfortingly cool – but never put these in the freezer, as it makes them far too cold for sensitive gums. You can also get

teething gels, but my favourite treatment is the homeopathic remedy Camomila, which I find can take the edge off the pain and discomfort.

FOOD AND DRINKS TO SOOTHE

You may find that a teething baby goes off his food and only wants cool liquids, or perhaps just cool foods, either hard or soft. Any foods will almost certainly need to be soft and easy to swallow. Yoghurt straight from the fridge with, say, mashed banana or fruit purée, chilled rice pudding (with a little honey if your baby is over 12 months), or for a 10-month-plus baby, a little cold soft ripe papaya or my fruit jellies can all work well, as can good-quality ice-cream. Even carrot purée with a little hummus

---

MEDICINE CHEST – SOOTHING FOODS FOR TEETHING BABIES

- **Yoghurt**
- **Mashed banana**
- **Fruit purée**
- **Chilled rice pudding with honey**
- **Soft ripe papaya**
- **Fruit jelly (see page 163)**
- **Risotto**
- **Pasta with a little oil**
- **Puréed vegetables**

or olive oil or some bolognaise sauce is worth a try. If your baby seems to like the softer texture, try a simple risotto, or – once your baby is ready for the texture – white pasta with a little olive oil and puréed vegetables, such as pumpkin or carrot.

Older babies sometimes prefer dry, hard foods such as toast or oat biscuits to try to cut their teeth on. You just have to play around with different textures and temperatures to find what really works and soothes your baby – there's no hard and fast rule.

PAINKILLERS

Liquid paracetamol can be a lifesaver if your baby really needs pain relief. There are times when complementary or natural remedies may not be enough, and as long as the instructions are followed, there's nothing wrong with conventional medicine.

Note that you must not give aspirin or any medicine containing aspirin to any child under 16 years old, except on the specific recommendation of a doctor, because of the possibility of extremely serious – even potentially fatal – adverse effects (a condition called Reye's syndrome.)

TODDLERS WITH TOOTH DECAY

Eating a diet rich in sugar and starch increases the risk of tooth decay. The best way to keep teeth in good condition and prevent decay is to ensure that you help your toddler to clean them regularly to get rid of any plaque build-up.

LOOKING AFTER YOUR BABY'S OR TODDLER'S TEETH

Prevention is better than cure, so in order to keep your baby's teeth healthy and free from decay, dentists say you should:

- Clean his teeth at least twice a day to prevent plaque build-up. Brush his teeth for 2 minutes. They say any longer and you're not getting rid of any more plaque.

- Use a toothpaste containing fluoride – you can buy good baby toothpastes.

- Take him for a dental check-up every 6 or 12 months.

- Floss between his teeth once he has a few milk teeth. After eating or drinking acidic food or drink, such as fruit, fruit juice or fizzy drink, you should wait an hour before cleaning his teeth. By brushing straight away, you are rubbing the acid into the enamel – which makes things worse.

If your toddler is suffering from toothache, the chances are that one of his teeth is decaying. You should take him to the dentist as soon as possible, as there's also the possibility the pain may be due to something more serious. If you can't get an immediate dental appointment and your toddler's toothache seems very painful, you can try giving the appropriate dose of a painkiller such as paracetamol – but do not give aspirin.

coughs and colds

Colds and coughs are par for the course for all babies and toddlers. As tough as they are for everyone, they are important because they help a child get his immune response mechanism right.

DRUGS AND MEDICAL TREATMENTS

We must allow children to fight these infections as much as possible without taking drugs.

However, if you have any concerns over their breathing, if they're off their food or have a fever of over 39°C (102°F), seek medical help within 24 hours. A baby under 8 weeks old should be seen within a few hours if he has any of these symptoms.

VIRAL INFECTIONS

Most common colds and coughs are caused by a virus, which is why doctors are reluctant (and quite rightly so) to prescribe antibiotics, which only zap bacterial infections.

We can help ease our child's symptoms and we can make his immune system stronger and less vulnerable to coughs and colds by looking to food and a few natural remedies.

EATING FOR IMMUNITY: BABIES

The key nutrients for the development of an efficient immune system are zinc, selenium and vitamins A, C and E. These are in plentiful supply in formula milk (as its vitamin and mineral content is constant and set at the right levels), and most likely in breast milk. Breast milk also has additional immune system-boosting powers that are unique to it (see page 17).

If you're breast-feeding, it is worth checking through the list of these key nutrients to ensure you're taking in enough

COUGHS AND COLDS MEDICINE CHEST

- **Do give babies, especially those who are bottle fed, plenty of cooled boiled water.**

- **Do feed babies over 6 months foods rich in vitamin A, C and E (see pages 76-77).**

- **Do feed babies over 6 months foods rich in zinc and selenium (see page 77).**

- **Don't increase your baby's milk instead of giving more water.**

- **Don't give your baby juice instead of water.**

of the foods that are not only going to help your child, but also you, resist or fight coughs and colds.

EATING FOR IMMUNITY: 6+MONTHS

If your child is over 6 months old, it is a good idea to increase his intake of foods that contain immune-boosting nutrients – zinc, selenium and vitamins A, C, and E. This is especially important if you've noticed that he's succumbing to coughs and colds more often than other babies, or is less able to shake them off.

WATER

Make sure a baby with a cough or cold drinks plenty of fluids from the moment the illness starts, especially if he's running a temperature. Seek medical advice if he becomes dehydrated, as this is very serious for babies (see page 216 for the symptoms of dehydration).

It is especially important to give extra water to bottle-fed babies; breast-fed babies are able to take more milk (hence fluid) in their breast-feeds (although they still benefit from extra water when ill). Don't dilute formula, thinking they need more water, as they still need the nutrients in the milk powder – you need to get the extra water into them just as plain boiled water.

Remember that babies won't have a problem with plain water – you don't need to and shouldn't use juice (even the so-called baby ones), as they'll develop a hard-to-break sweet tooth and will be taking in unnecessary sugars, and perhaps sweeteners, additives and preservatives. Persevere with giving them water and they'll soon adjust to it.

FRUIT TO HEAL

The old saying 'feed a cold' is true, as nutrient-rich foods enable babies and toddlers to fight bugs.

When babies are over 6 months, it's important to keep tempting them with little bits of immune-boosting, vitamin C-rich foods (so long as they're up to eating). Vitamin C is one of the most important antioxidant vitamins, and can help your baby recover more quickly and prevent him getting another bug straight afterwards, which can happen if his immune system is challenged by the cold virus.

Puréed vitamin C-rich fruit is ideal from 6 months. For 7-month-olds onwards, a fresh fruit smoothie (dilute it half and half with water) is good. Once he's old enough to have chunks of fruit (usually around 10 months), a few pieces of kiwi fruit are good, as they can be soothing to suck, especially if they're cold.

Sneak lots of vitamin C into his food – for example, crush blueberries or raspberries into cereal or pudding rice, or mash them on toast soldiers. Although they're lower in vitamin C than blueberries, kiwis and oranges, I find satsumas, clementines, and mandarins are always a hit (but should be avoided by babies under 7 months or those who aren't ready for the texture). Don't overdo it though, as too many can cause an upset tummy.

HONEY TO HEAL

For babies over 12 months, honey can be brilliant for sore throats – it not only soothes, but can help them recover from the virus quicker because of its strong antibacterial and general immune-system-boosting properties. A little honey in a lemon drink often goes down well and gives them a good dose of vitamin C too. A little pot of yoghurt and honey (especially Manuka honey) can be a real nourishing therapy too. But remember that honey is not suitable for babies under 12 months.

GARLIC TO HEAL

For toddlers who can cope with strong flavours, fresh garlic helps combat infections. Toddlers with a sore throat may be willing to drink a crushed garlic clove in a mug of warm milk (cow's, breast, soya, oat, rice, formula, etc.). Bear in mind that babies should only drink cow's milk as a drink after the age of 12 months. Note that you should avoid using garlic oil, aged garlic extract and garlic powders because, unlike fresh garlic, these forms of garlic have few healing properties.

DON'T AVOID DAIRY

There is no scientific evidence to show that dairy products are mucus-forming and therefore should be avoided if your child has a cough or cold. Babies need the nutrients that milk and dairy offer (unless they have an intolerance or allergy, of course), so they can still eat dairy products.

'It's a good idea to increase intake of foods that contain immune-boosting nutrients – selenium, zinc, and vitamins A, C and E.'

diarrhoea

Babies and toddlers can develop diarrhoea for many different reasons. If your baby passes runny stools twice or more in a row, or intermittently in 24 hours, he probably has diarrhoea – but bear in mind that breast-fed babies in particular often have very loose, semi-fluid poos and this isn't the same as diarrhoea.

BABIES WITH DIARRHOEA

Babies with diarrhoea are prone to dehydration, unless you're able to keep their fluid intake up. But make sure they're not drinking too much fruit juice, as the sugar in the juice can itself lead to diarrhoea. See the box opposite for how to prevent dehydration, but if they're suffering from any of the following symptoms, you should phone your GP immediately.

- If they're abnormally drowsy or irritable.
- If they refuse their feed for 6 hours or more.
- If they've been vomiting for 6 hours or more.
- If their eyes are sunken, or they're passing only small amounts of urine.

When babies start eating foods they haven't had before, their stools can become runny. Their digestive system may not break down the new food completely, and there may be undigested bits in the stools. Keep trying small amounts of the new foods and the gut should soon adapt. A lot of mucus in the stools is an indication that the gut may be having a problem breaking the food down, so lay off that food for a couple of weeks or try mashing or puréeing the food to make it easier to digest.

TODDLERS WITH DIARRHOEA

Sometimes a toddler who is otherwise healthy starts passing watery poos, frequently containing pieces of recognizable foods such as peas and carrots. This type of toddler's diarrhoea isn't serious; it could be simply that his gut has trouble digesting a new food or dealing with the quantities of foods you're giving him, or that he's having too much of one type of food such as beans and lentils. Try to make his diet more varied.

DIARRHOEA MEDICINE CHEST

- **Do give him lots of fluids.**
- **Do take him to the doctor if he shows other adverse symptoms.**
- **Do give him live bio-yoghurt.**
- **Do give him pectin-rich foods such as apples and carrots.**
- **Don't give him significant amounts of dairy.**

FOODS THAT CAN UPSET TUMMIES

There's no reason why a baby's gut can't tolerate spices, but sometimes they may have loose stools to start with. If you start putting oil or butter in his food, or cheese in vegetable purées, the change in fat levels may trigger a little short-term diarrhoea. Dried fruits, although they are great for babies, contain a lot of sugar, which can unsettle a young gut.

FOOD POISONING

If you suspect that your child may have food poisoning, see your GP. Food-poisoning symptoms such as diarrhoea and vomiting start after a few hours, although occasionally it can take days before the bacteria have reproduced enough in your child's body to make him ill. It's best to keep children away from playgroup, nursery or the childminder when they have diarrhoea because the bugs can spread incredibly easily.

If you think your child may have food-poisoning, it's best to stick to water and simple dry foods, such as rice cakes, plain dry toast and plain rice.

Many types of food-poisoning bugs are resistant to antibiotics and tend to clear up by themselves. Don't be too eager to give your baby antibiotics, as sometimes the body needs to be allowed to fight and build up immune strength on its own. However, sometimes they are necessary, so discuss the pros and cons with your GP.

DEHYDRATION

When children have diarrhoea or feel sick, there's little point in forcing them to eat. What you need to remember is that getting fluid down them is essential. To keep your child's electrolyte balance healthy, give him rehydration fluids. You can buy these from the pharmacy.

To help rebalance the body's electrolytes and prevent any dehydration symptoms such as a sunken fontanel, give small amounts of rehydrating solution every couple of hours while there are signs of diarrhoea.

BREAST-FED BABIES AND DIARRHOEA

Continue breast-feeding if your baby has diarrhoea, as it can shorten the course of the illness by favourably altering the bowel's bacterial balance. Breast milk also contains antibodies and substances

YOUR BABY'S FLUID REQUIREMENT

Every baby needs to drink between 500ml and 1,500ml of fluid a day, depending on his weight.

Weight (kg)	Fluid requirement (ml per day)
Under 4kg	500ml
4kg	600ml
6kg	900ml
7kg	1,050ml
8kg	1,200ml
9kg	1,350ml
over 10kg	1,500ml

such as mucin that help protect babies against intestinal infections. Although breast milk is relatively high in lactose, it doesn't seem to trouble babies recovering from a bout of diarrhoea.

FORMULA-FED BABIES AND DIARRHOEA

If your baby is fed on an ordinary cow's milk formula, you may find that swapping to either a casein hydrolysate or soya formula (see pages 30-31) can help reduce his diarrhoea. It may be that the lactose or cow's milk protein in the formula is aggravating his gut. Your doctor, however, may suggest that you just give rehydration fluids, or dilute his feed. Don't dilute formula without your doctor's or health visitor's supervision.

AS HE STARTS TO GET BETTER

When your baby starts to improve and you want to give him something solid, opt for rice cakes, freshly cooked rice, rice pudding (made with water, or milk if you don't think he's sensitive to it), porridge, a piece of dry toast or mashed papaya or banana, depending on his age. Mashed potato works well too, but don't add any oil or butter – any kind of fat can aggravate the gut.

WATCH THE DAIRY PRODUCE

When your child is getting over a diarrhoea or sickness bug, his body can become temporarily intolerant of dairy. However, for babies over 7 months, live bio yoghurt is the exception – it contains natural bacteria such as lactobacillus and bifida that can help him recover.

Antibiotics often take away all the good bacteria from the gut as well as the bad, and a little live probiotic yoghurt each day for a couple of weeks can help put the healthy ones back. Live bio yoghurt can also help prevent tummy bugs and improve your child's ability to digest food. Try giving him just a little to start with, perhaps with some honey drizzled over if he's over 12 months.

NATURE'S BINDER – PECTIN

Pectin is a form of soluble fibre found in fruits and vegetables, especially apples, carrots, rice and bananas. It can help reduce diarrhoea by absorbing water and important minerals in the bowel. Give 6-month-old babies apple purée with a little rice. If your baby's old enough, give him a piece of raw carrot or unskinned apple. You could mix in a teaspoon of carob powder, a traditional herbal remedy for diarrhoea. Grated carrot and apple is another option.

Apple juice, diluted, can contain a lot of useful pectin – but go back to plain water as soon as he's better. Blueberries are good, not only because they contain pectin, but also because they contain anthocyanosides, which have a mild antibiotic action.

PROTECT HIS BOTTOM

Diarrhoea can be miserable, especially for babies in nappies, so protect and soothe bottoms with a chamomile or comfrey ointment. And try to give your baby's bottom some nappy-free time, exposed to the air, several times a day.

yummy parent

A crucial part of being a good mum is looking after yourself. It's easy be so attentive to your child's life and wellbeing – and, if you're a working mum, to your job as well – that there's little time left for you.

In this chapter you'll find lots of practical ideas about maximizing how you feel physically and emotionally, from easy recipe ideas to help you eat properly when you've missed the supermarket and have to make something from leftovers, to suggestions for getting back in shape after the birth and for how to keep up when you've got a toddler who's 'into everything'.

But this chapter isn't just for mums, it's also for dads. Many men look after their children too, and they can just as easily find that their body has 'lost its way' when a child comes into their life, even if they're not actively involved in the day-to-day childcare. So my tips are for any adult involved in parenting – including grandparents and other relatives, nannies and childminders.

food and drink

It often takes no more effort to prepare two meals than one, and then freeze or refrigerate the spare for later. It's also a good idea to use internet shopping to keep stocked up with food.

breakfast

It can be hard to find time for food first thing in the morning but breakfast is a time to get nourishment inside the whole family – including you. How you start the day will be affected by how old your child is – you might munch toast while breast-feeding, or sit down with your toddler, both of you tucking into cereal.

Even if you're not much of a breakfast eater or aren't ready to eat at the same time as your child, you can wait until she's gone to playgroup or is being looked after by a relative or childminder.

BREAST-FEEDING MUMS
Make yourself a fruit smoothie or a milk shake (ideally with some yoghurt or banana) using milk of any sort. Try my raspberry and soya shake (see page 158). Milk will give you more sustenance than apple juice, although that's good too.

PARENTS OF OLDER BABIES
Try to make time in the morning to sit down with your child – even if you don't have much of an appetite. It gives her the message that eating together is important, and that you are important too. If she sees you just grabbing bites while doing other things, it can be confusing.

PREPARING FOR THE DAY
If you're feeling on top of things, you can think about preparing the evening meal at this time, especially if you have a slow cooker.

EASY, NOURISHING BREAKFASTS

1 Porridge with honey or some fresh or dried fruits. Try making it with toasted oat flakes too – toast them gently under the grill and use in the same way as raw oats.

2 Wholemeal toast with peanut butter and banana (if you have a family history of nut allergy and are breast-feeding, use good-quality, high-fruit, low-sugar marmalade or jam/pure fruit spread). Alternatively, spread on some fish pâté (page 135).

3 Home-made muesli with fresh fruit or natural yoghurt, or some dried fruit compote (page 106) with ricotta.

4 Scrambled eggs on wholegrain toast – eggs contain every essential amino acid the body needs. Alternatively, try my eggy bread with fruits (page 157) or a creamy mushroom omelette.

5 A couple of oatcakes with a little butter and pure fruit spread, and a glass of milk. Try apple and pear, or blackcurrant, black cherry or blackberry spreads.

snacks

NUTRITIOUS SNACKS

1 Rice cakes – OK, the salt-free ones are technically healthiest, but I just don't like them without a little salt. If your diet is generally low-salt because your child needs it to be, I think a little salted rice cake is fine. They're certainly better than the sugary ones.

2 Dried fruits, ideally organic.

3 Unsalted nuts.

4 Unsalted/plain popcorn – either bought or home-made (see right).

5 A small bottle of fresh fruit smoothie – the ready-made brand I prefer contains only fresh fruit and has no added sugar. A good smoothie can give you a tasty energizing drink, but they may give you a bit of a sugar high if you're sensitive, so I dilute mine with some water.

Snacks are a lifesaver for me – it's good to have something in my bag and the car, in case the day goes mad. My favourites are the obvious: fruit – especially apples, pears, tangerines, satsumas – that doesn't get squashed if you throw toys into the bag on top of it. I also carry unsalted nuts and dried fruits (ideally organic and therefore unsulphured) – Medjool dates can lift my energy just enough to get through a few more hours,

and can stop me from crashing during the 5–6pm zone, when many parents find they're exhausted, especially if they have a young baby who's colicky in the evening. Having nutritious snacks to hand can help you avoid biscuits, crisps and chocolates – not to mention the 5pm glass of wine! Try slices of sticky fig and apple cake (page 177), banana and walnut loaf cake (page 172) or something lighter like dried fruit compote and yoghurt. Fruit bars (page 174) or bought cereal bars are also good.

HOMEMADE POPCORN

Small knob of butter
Corn

1 Melt the butter in a medium-sized non-stick saucepan (you can make it without butter, but I prefer the flavour with just a little). Add just enough corn to cover the bottom of the pan in a single layer. Cover with a tight lid.

2 Turn up the heat and stay by the pan, shaking it back and forth, until you hear the corn start to pop. Turn the heat down and continue shaking for another couple of minutes.

3 Allow the popcorn to cool a little before eating. You can store it for a few days in an airtight container.

lunch

You need refuelling just as much as your child does. Sit down with her at lunchtime, making a portion for yourself – or if she's still young enough to have a lunchtime nap, use the time to prepare a good lunch for yourself. A hot meal at lunchtime can work well, as this is usually when you're less tired and therefore have more energy and inclination to make something nutritious. A good lunch can give you the energy and emotional strength to tackle the rest of the day. The recipes in this book are perfect for all the family.

QUICK LUNCHES

If you're on your own or don't want a substantial cooked meal, you could try a simple omelette or a bowl of soup (see pages 110–111) and some wholegrain bread – and there's nothing wrong with a home-made sandwich. If you need something sweet afterwards, have fresh fruit or yoghurt, or a couple of dried fruits with a cup of tea.

EASY LUNCHES FOR WHEN YOU'RE CHILD-FREE

1 Tinned cream of tomato soup with wholegrain toast. I make mine go further and taste less sweet by adding half a tin of chopped tomatoes to each tin of soup. Tinned tomato soup can contain more tomatoes, less salt and therefore be more nutritious than so-called fresh ready-made soups – and it's a lot cheaper.

2 Hummus (bought or home-made, page 113) and cucumber sandwich made with wholegrain bread. (There's nothing wrong with white bread if you don't have any wholegrain – it doesn't have as much fibre but it's still a good lunch option.)

3 Sardines or mackerel mashed with a little lemon and black pepper on toast – a great high-protein, omega-oil-rich lunch (and see my fish pâté recipes, page 135). Wholegrain bread is best – or you could warm some pitta bread and slice tomatoes and cucumber into it with a few rocket leaves.

4 Good cold meats, such as prosciutto, with salad and a sliced avocado –throw tinned beans into the salad if you like, to add some fibre. Season well, with plenty of lemon juice, black pepper and any fresh herbs to hand.

5 A piece of cheese with some oatcakes and fresh fruit or crisp celery sticks. Cutting the rind off soft cheeses reduces the fat content and therefore the calories, if you want to lose a little pregnancy or parenting weight.

And try my salads on pages 116–121.

dinner

Parents these days seem more likely to eat separately from their children at the end of the day. Extended working days mean partners return home much later, and unless you're a Mediterranean late-night-eating family, the kids usually eat together and then parents eat after the children are in bed.

LATE DINNERS ALONE

If you're going to be eating later, try to sit down with your child to encourage her to eat at the table. Take the few minutes while she's eating to have a

---

EASY DINNERS FOR WHEN YOUR BABY IS IN BED

pasta – with finely grated Parmesan cheese, fresh rocket (bagged is fine), sliced tomatoes and a glug of good olive oil. See also pages 152–153 for other pasta recipes.

steamed veggies and hummus – broccoli, purple sprouting, green beans, carrots, fennel, courgettes, etc. – in a bowl with a big dollop of hummus on top.

baked fresh fish (see box, right) – frozen fish can be a very good option, and see also my recipe for cod with roasted tomatoes (page 131).

butternut squash salad (see the box on page 229)

quick creamy mushroom omelette (see the box on page 229).

BAKED FISH

1 piece of tuna or salmon per person
olive oil
freshly ground black pepper
fresh herbs – e.g. tarragon, basil, parsley, coriander (but not mint, sage or rosemary, as they're too strong), chopped
1 lemon or lime

1 Preheat the oven to 200°C/400°F/gas mark 6.
2 Take a piece of foil big enough to wrap three times around the fish and pop the fish in the middle. Drizzle with a little olive oil, then sprinkle with some pepper and the herbs. Either squeeze over a little lemon or lime juice or pop a couple of slices on top of the fish.
3 Seal the fish into a foil parcel. Pop into the oven for 10 minutes or until cooked thoroughly, and serve with salad, veggies, potatoes, rice, couscous, etc.

---

healthy snack yourself – a bowl of soup, a simple salad, fresh or dried fruits, a smoothie, even a cup of tea with a banana, or a piece of cheese and an apple or pear – these will give you the energy both to get through the time until she goes to bed and to cook something nutritious for yourself later on.

Parents who expect to go until 9pm without a late afternoon snack often hit a brick wall and find cooking too much effort.

LAST-MINUTE PASTA

Pasta is always a good standby for when you have to conjure up dinner at the last minute. Here, I have included three suggestions for good, quick pasta dinners. I think pasta is always best cooked *al dente* (with bite, not mushy) but if you prefer it softer, then simply cook it for a bit longer.

Serve the cooked pasta with finely grated Parmesan cheese (cheese grated from a block of Parmesan is far better than the dried variety), olive oil, black pepper, and even a couple of chopped anchovies.

If you have a squash or pumpkin, roast in a hot oven for 30 minutes or so until golden brown and soft, then peel the flesh away. Mix it with cooked pasta and cheese for a sweet and satisfying meal.

Mix cooked pasta with some well-drained butter beans, a little lemon juice, a couple of handfuls of freshly chopped parsley and a few chopped olives.

LAST-MINUTE RICE

Rice is another winner – use it to make a simple risotto. Choose Arborio rice if you have it, otherwise opt for short-grain pudding rice, which is a good substitute. Stock cubes are fine, and preferably use dried mushrooms such as porcini (I wouldn't use tinned mushrooms, as they taste very processed). I use dried mushrooms in the risotto and then add a few fresh button mushrooms just before it's ready. Risotto made with frozen peas with some fresh mint thrown in at the end is delicious.

LAST-MINUTE LENTILS

You shouldn't forget daal (see page 148). Even if you're not vegetarian, you should try this – it's probably the ultimate comfort food. All of the ingredients for daal should be readily available, and it's even better when reheated. Serve it with warm bread, such as chapatti.

APPETITE AND FEELING

It's easy to slip into not having the motivation to eat properly when you feel low. But try to nibble on some fruit and force yourself to eat something nourishing, even if you don't have much of an appetite. Also, pick up the phone and talk to a close friend – they may be able to cook you something, or do some shopping for you, and if you're really not up to getting out to the shops and don't have anyone easily around to help out, get on the computer or the phone and get a supermarket delivery – many of them can deliver within 24 hours.

BUTTERNUT SQUASH SALAD

Serves 2

1 butternut squash
olive oil
a handful of hazelnuts
1 avocado, sliced
a few handfuls of washed watercress
a few handfuls of washed rocket
1 buffalo mozzarella, torn
hazelnut oil
apple vinegar
dijon mustard
freshly ground black pepper

1 Preheat the oven to 100°C/350°F/gas mark 4.
2 Slice the butternut squash in half, remove the seeds, drizzle with olive oil, place in the oven and roast for 40 minutes or until the crust has turned a good nutty brown and the flesh is soft.
3 10 minutes before cooking time's up, scatter the hazelnuts on a baking tray and roast at the bottom of the oven until they are warmed through and turning just a little darker (be careful they don't burn).
4 Remove the squash from the oven, scoop out the flesh in large pieces and place in a salad bowl. Tie up the hazelnuts in a plastic bag and crush lightly with a rolling pin.
5 To your salad bowl add the avocado, watercress, rocket and mozzarella. Make a dressing with 2 parts olive oil, 1 part hazelnut oil, 1 part apple vinegar and a little Dijon mustard. Add to the salad with lots of black pepper, and sprinkle with the nuts. Serve while the squash is still warm.

QUICK CREAMY MUSHROOM OMELETTE

Serves 1

3 large free-range eggs
freshly ground black pepper
10g/¼oz of freshly grated Parmesan or mature Cheddar, grated
a knob of butter
50g/2oz of mushrooms, sliced
1 dessertspoon of single cream

1 Beat the eggs in a bowl. Add a couple of big twists of black pepper and the Parmesan or Cheddar, and beat lightly.
2 Melt a tiny knob of butter in a small pan over a medium heat, add the mushrooms and fry for about 5 minutes, until they turn soft and darker. Turn the heat right down for a minute, then add the cream. Keep warm on a very low heat.
3 In a small non-stick frying pan, melt another tiny knob of butter. When it's foamy, add the egg mixture and turn the heat as low as possible. Preheat the grill.
4 Once the eggs have set and thickened and only the top is runny (which should take about 5–8 minutes), spoon the mushroom mixture on to the omelette and pop the frying pan under the preheated grill for about 30 seconds, until the top of the omelette has set.
5 Serve with salad, or some cooked beans or broccoli and scoop the omelette up with fresh wholegrain bread or warm wholemeal pitta bread.

drinks

I go through periods when I try not to have any alcohol because when I'm really tired, even a single glass can send my energy levels so low that I just want to crawl into bed. I also find my sleep, when I get it, can be less nourishing (alcohol disrupts REM sleep, which is the one we really need), making the next day a struggle. And as I get older I find my tolerance for even the smallest amounts of alcohol gets worse – I'm definitely a cheap date now!

But then there'll be a day when Maya's gone to bed, the house is quiet, and a glass of wine is what my body craves and actually needs in order to relax. It's when the odd glass becomes half a bottle or more, or you find yourself pouring the wine out of habit, or you're not bothered about the taste of the wine but simply want something in your hand when you sit down that perhaps it's time to look again at your drinking.

HOW TO AVOID DRINKING TOO MUCH

One way I've managed to stop myself reaching for a glass of wine every night is to have a shower or bath as soon as Maya has gone to bed. This not only puts a block on a behaviour that so often is habitual, but a warming bath or shower can often relax me even more than a drink, helps me sleep well and saves the hangover!

But note that if you have a steaming hot bath and then decide to have a glass of wine, you will need to drink even more water, as you will have probably sweated a lot and can get drunk very easily.

If you've been struggling with tiredness, try cutting out alcohol for a couple of weeks – I can virtually guarantee that you will feel much more energized at the end of your time of abstinence.

Watch out for alcohol's appetite-stimulating effects. An aperitif works big-time on tired parents – a glass can not only make you feel more hungry so you eat a larger portion, but can also cloud your resolve not to overeat, and overeating at night can not only disturb your sleep, it can lead to your piling on the weight if it becomes a habit.

TEA

Chamomile tea is good for unwinding and de-stressing, as are lemon verbena, lemon balm, and fresh mint tea.

To make mint tea, just put a few sprigs of fresh mint into a teapot, top up with boiling water, leave for a couple of minutes and pour – utter heaven, and great too for an over-tired gut that feels acidic and not much like eating.

losing pregnancy weight

MY 10-STEP WEIGHT-LOSS PLAN

I'm not going to tell you exactly what to eat and when, as I don't think this works best for new parents. Instead, I want to talk you through a basic style of eating that should help you to lose 2–3kg in a couple of weeks. Everyone's different, and you may not see the weight dropping off instantly. But stick to this plan and after two weeks you should see an improvement. But note that the plan should be followed for only two weeks, and you must consult your GP first if you are on any medication.

DRINK WATER

Drink 2.5 litres of water (tap, bottled, fizzy, hot, cold or with a herbal teabag in it) every day. A glass an hour is a good way to spread this out. Initially, you may need to go to the loo every ten minutes while your body readjusts itself to proper hydration, but it's worth it: water improves digestion by getting things moving in the body. You'll also feel more energized, and you'll be able to concentrate better. Water also swells the food you eat, so helps your brain recognize when you've eaten enough. However, you shouldn't drink flavoured fizzy drinks: they have more calories than water and don't hydrate you as well. You should also avoid alcohol (which not only has lots of calories but also tends to dehydrate you) and have tea and coffee no more than twice a day.

BREAST-FEEDING MUMS

If you're breast-feeding, you should find you start to lose weight gradually, as long as you're eating a healthy balanced diet. You shouldn't go on a strict crash weight-loss diet while breast-feeding, as you can quickly find that your milk supply or quality diminishes and you can end up physically and mentally exhausted. (See pages 21–25 for how to eat healthily and still lose a little weight while breast-feeding.)

If you're not breast-feeding, the basic mantra is to eat healthily and exercise regularly, as this will ensure the weight comes off in a way that preserves your metabolic rate – crash diets usually end up being followed by a weight gain that's even more than you started with.

HEALTHY SNACKS

Snack on fruit – fill a big bowl and put it where you'll notice it. Unsalted nuts are good too, but just a few at a time because they are high in calories – and watch you don't leave them around, as small children can easily choke. Another good snack is raw vegetables (e.g. cherry tomatoes, carrots or celery) with a little natural yoghurt, fresh mint and garlic. Or a bowl of soup can distract you from the biscuits or chunks of cheese.

VEGETABLES FOR LUNCH OR DINNER

At lunch and supper have a big portion of vegetables, steamed or lightly boiled, or an easy-to-grab bagged salad. You can even have half an avocado in a salad; this makes it creamy and you need less olive oil (which is fine but ensure that you only use a dessertspoonful per person per salad). You can eat plenty of vegetables (frozen ones can be useful. Avoid potatoes and sweet potatoes, but other root vegetables such as carrots and parsnips (which make great soups) are fine.

LIMIT COOKING FAT

Use only a little olive oil or butter with your vegetables, and add lemon juice, fresh herbs, and plenty of black pepper to give food extra flavour.

EAT LEAN PROTEIN

For lunch and supper choose a lean protein food, such as lean steak, chicken (including the skin, because it can be a bit bland without), fish (oily and non-oily), seafood, eggs, game, etc. You need a lot of energy being a parent, so I wouldn't skimp too much on the portion size of these lean proteins – for example, a large breast of chicken, a small steak, a slightly larger piece of fish, a couple of eggs, or six large prawns are fine at each meal. But it's important to eat slowly and savour your food, because this helps your body have enough time to register when you've had enough. Eating too quickly usually causes you to eat too much and to feel bloated and uncomfortable afterwards.

PREPARING FOR MY 10-STEP PLAN

• Allow yourself a day to stock up on the foods you'll need.

• If you have friends – maybe other mums – who want to do the plan, why not club together to ensure that you have lots of good food around when you meet up for coffee, and make a pact so that no one sabotages you by doing a chocolate run?

IF YOU WEAKEN

There will, of course, be times when you're climbing the walls – not because you aren't eating enough to live on, but because you're eating less than your body is used to. To help you through these times, try the following:

• Drink water, or herbal tea if you need something more comforting, and the hunger should go away.

• Distract yourself: think positive, visualize yourself thinner and trimmer, and imagine how well you will feel after two weeks.

• If you are overcome by a sugar craving, sniffing a bottle of vanilla essence or sprinkling a little cinnamon on your cappuccino can make it go away.

EAT A GOOD BREAKFAST

Start the day with a good wholegrain or porridge-style breakfast (see page 106). Stir in a dollop of yoghurt plus a dribble of honey and a small mashed banana or grated apple and a handful of raisins for sweetness. An alternative is two small pieces of wholegrain toast or bread, with a little butter and pure fruit spread. Apart from this breakfast, avoid bread, rice, pasta, potatoes, cereals, oats, etc.

If you really want something starch-like, have a cup of cooked beans or lentils with your proteins and other vegetables. Add them to salads, soups, casseroles, or just drizzle them with a little olive or hemp oil, some lemon juice and fresh herbs.

LIMIT CHEESE AND MAYONNAISE

Avoid mayonnaise, large amounts of cheese, creamy sauces and anything fried or battered. You don't need to go low-fat – your baby needs full cream milk, yoghurt, etc., so this would mean that you would have to buy two different types of products. Instead, just have a small amount of the full-fat version.

AVOID SWEET FOODS

Avoid sweet foods apart from fresh fruit – raw or cooked. No biscuits, cakes, or chocolates. Puddings (see pages 160–171) should be fresh fruit. You could add raspberries, strawberries, mangoes or pineapples for an exotic twist. A little fromage frais or natural yoghurt on top is fine. Don't exceed four portions of fresh fruit a day; it contains fruit sugar, which in excess could hinder weight loss.

WATCH YOUR PORTIONS

Serve half what you'd normally have, eat it slowly and then, if you need extra,

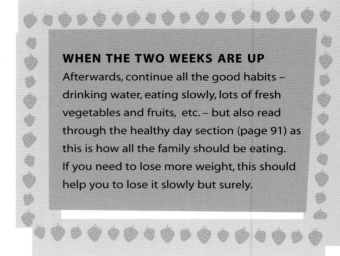

WHEN THE TWO WEEKS ARE UP
Afterwards, continue all the good habits – drinking water, eating slowly, lots of fresh vegetables and fruits, etc. – but also read through the healthy day section (page 91) as this is how all the family should be eating. If you need to lose more weight, this should help you to lose it slowly but surely.

have it, but stop when you're full. If you find that difficult, try imagining someone saying 'Surely that's enough.'

WILLPOWER NEEDED

You need this when your body is crying, 'I'm hungry!' and the diet seems not to be working. It will, if you hang in there.

sleep

The one thing that all parents – mums and dads – complain about is tiredness due to lack of sleep. This is especially problematic with young babies who need feeding during the night but even older babies and toddlers disrupt their parents' sleep. I know that I get so over-tired that I struggle to go to sleep even though I know my body desperately needs to. It's had me in tears at times. (Mind you, crying can be a good sleep trigger.) These are my tips for cajoling the body into a slumber state.

MILK AND HERB TEAS

Research shows that milk – either cold or warm – can aid sleep. If you don't like plain milk, you can add a little cocoa powder or chocolate but don't add too much because they contain caffeine-like substances. Chamomile tea can also be effective in helping sleep.

HERBAL REMEDIES

It's easy to assume that since herbs are natural, they're always safe to use. But herbs can be as powerful as some over-the-counter or prescription drugs – some are even potentially toxic – so don't just assume they're safe to take. However, as long as you use good-quality herbs, the ones in the box (above) are safe and will help you sleep; they are all fine for breast-feeding mums. They can all be taken as tablets or as a liquid tincture.

HERBS THAT ARE SAFE FOR BREAST-FEEDING MUMS:

- **gentle chamomile**
- **small amounts of passionflower and valerian** (these will calm the central nervous system and thought processes)
- **wild lettuce**
- **californian poppy**

PZIZZ MACHINES

You could also check out Pzizz machines. These are NLP (neurolinguistic programming), ipod-lookalike devices and are one of the best ways to relax I've come across. You literally plug yourself into the device and listen to a digitalized system of noises, music, voice, etc., for about 10–15 minutes. It can be extremely effective at helping you to relax and sleep – and I also find it great for rejuvenating me during the day! Check them out on the internet – you can buy them in the USA.

SLEEP FOODS

Late at night avoid very sweet foods, such as biscuits and chocolate, cheese and meat. But starchy carbohydrates – bread, potatoes, couscous, pasta and rice – encourage the brain to produce serotonin, a natural sleep-inducer.

index

AUTHOR'S ACKNOWLEDGMENTS

As a working mum, there is no way I could do the work I do, the work I love (including writing this book, which I have to say was a bit of a tall order with Maya starting her new school just as pen was about to hit paper!) without the love and support of my very special family and friends – you know who you are and although I don't get around to saying it out loud very often, this is one of those times when I do. So thank you for being the best family and friends anyone could ever wish for, whilst I just want to thank in particular Martin, Marcela, Tessa, Terry, and Nadine, and last but no means least, Lesja and John.

A special thank you to Jools Oliver for her very kind foreword, to my former agent, Lisa Sullivan, who has annoyingly (but good for her) returned to her native country, Australia.

For exceptional recipe testing and food styling, thanks to Annie Rigg and Louise Mackaness. Heartfelt thanks to Annie Lee for her second-to-none editing. Thanks also to Sarah Schenker and of course not forgetting Becca Spry for all her great input and care over this hard-to-deliver baby. Thanks to Nicky Collings and Deirdre Rooney for such lovely design and photos, and to Maggie Smith for (almost) hiding my wrinkles and bags.

Thank you to Michelle at Suzy Harper for the gorgeous clothes. Thanks also to my friend and great colleague Louise Plank for all her support, hard work and belief, whilst not forgetting Dominic, my newly found fantastic assistant, for getting me through the final stages of this book.

Finally to Navin, whom we love dearly and shall always be indebted to forever.

PUBLISHER'S ACKNOWLEDGMENTS

Thanks to Tracey Cotterell and all the staff and parents at Southill Nursery for allowing us to photograph the babies and toddlers in their buildings, grounds, and at their organic vegetable patch.

Thanks to Diana Henry for helping to find some wonderful babies, including Alistair, Connie, Ellie, Evie May, George, Gracie, Jack, Lilyanna, Nicholas, Oliver, Olivia, Reuben, Rowan, and Rufus. Thanks also to any other baby models, and their parents, who kindly gave up their time.

The publisher would also like to thank Boots for the supply of baby items.